THE
BIG THICKET
OF TEXAS

THE
BIG THICKET
OF TEXAS

America's Ecological Wonder

HOWARD PEACOCK

WITH PHOTOGRAPHS BY THE AUTHOR

LITTLE, BROWN AND COMPANY
BOSTON   TORONTO

FIRST EDITION

All photographs not
otherwise credited were taken
by Howard Peacock.

Library of Congress Cataloging in Publication Data

Peacock, Howard H., 1925–
  The Big Thicket of Texas.

  Summary: Text and illustrations present the history,
special characteristics, and folklore of the 3.5 million
acres of land in eastern Texas known as the Big Thicket.
  1. Big Thicket National Preserve (Tex.) — Juvenile
literature. [1. Big Thicket National Preserve (Tex.)
2. National parks and reserves] I. Title.
F392.H37P43   1984   976.4'157   84-1988
ISBN 0-316-69583-1

MU
*Published simultaneously in Canada
by Little, Brown & Company (Canada) Limited*

PRINTED IN THE UNITED STATES OF AMERICA

For my wife, Kitty

For Mickey Johnston, Geraldine Watson, Dr. Pete Gunter, and the late Alice Cashen, who led the final victorious efforts to establish America's first national preserve in the Big Thicket; and for Arthur Temple, who with foresight and patience saw the need for constructive exchange and good-will between two old adversaries — the timber industry and the conservation movement — thus helping to heal long-festering wounds for the ultimate benefit of all Americans, young and old alike, who love and respect nature

Foreword

THE LIFEBLOOD of the Big Thicket is water. During a rainy
season water stands for weeks on the flat clay-pan surface. Who
hunts or searches in those flatlands will wade ankle-deep, resting
on an occasional island after scattering the deer that bed down
on it. Long after the rainwaters recede, the baygalls, bellying down
under the weight of black gums and pin oaks, hold black water
and decaying leaves on their spongy bottoms. Old roads that wind
through the Thicket are punctuated by small ponds of water, the
home of black, button-sized tadpoles and the visiting place of the
long green-striped garter snakes that feed on them. Grassy clearings in the Thicket are poked with dynamite holes, the mark of
the turpentiners, who have blasted out the old fat-pine stumps
and left a clear-water niche for delicate algae and whirligigs.
Palmetto swamps spread out along the bayous, where the banks
glide down and disappear under the brown water, and oxbows
lie hidden beyond the creek banks, waiting for the overflowing
fresh water to come back to liven them again.

In the traditional Bear Hunters' Thicket of Hardin County —
the heartland of Big Thicket legends — the main flowing water
travels down Pine Island Bayou and Little Pine Island Bayou. The
two bayous join about five crow-flying miles from the Neches
and finally and sluggishly pour their grey burden into that river
on its way down to the Gulf. The minor waters are the creeks
and sloughs that drain the Thicket uplands and soggy flatlands

and feed the larger waters that feed the rivers that feed the seas. Many are narrow step-over creeks and drains that quit running during dry weather, leaving pockets of water smelling foul of decaying vegetation. These wind through the flatland in outrageous curves that almost meet themselves.

Some of these creek names tell old stories that the early settlers knew: Union Wells Creek, where old Warren Collins and the Jayhawkers hid out during the Civil War, and Bad Luck Creek, where Captain Kaiser finally burned them out. We can understand the origin of Mill Creek and Meetinghouse Branch, but what are the stories behind Yearling Tick Branch and Bull Tongue Creek? The wildlife that roamed the Thicket in the early days is commemorated in Doe Pond Creek, Wolf Gully, and Panther Branch, and the fruit that makes the best of all jellies is remembered in Mayhaw Slough.

The sweetest water in the Big Thicket is Village Creek, which flows clear and cool along the eastern edge of the Thicket down to the Neches. And there are long stretches of clear water running through thick woods that must look as it looked when the first settlers came, well over a hundred years ago. But there are other places that are cleared and terraced and built upon. Houses, shacks, and trailers perch upon the creek's banks. Pollutants, both individual and industrial, add their effluvia to the water's flow. And the quiet places so easy to find twenty years ago are rattled by increasing visitations by an increasing population.

There are moments, however, when on a brisk October morning one walks its soft and verdant banks — there are times when this clear flowing part of the Big Thicket affords a sense of peaceful and primitive immediacy. One feels separated for a while — even with the distant sounds from the highways and airways — from the steel and plastic of modern cities, from the sharp corners and raw edges of modern living. One is glad that such places survive, that we can afford them in our swarming world.

The Big Thicket is Howard Peacock's territory. He has worked and lived with it for many years. He has acted as a guide for those who needed help to see the Thicket with a clearer eye, to see the plants and wildlife that escape casual observation. He has taught courses about it and conducted seminars for those who would learn the biology and ecology of the Big Thicket. He has been constant in his labors to get the Big Thicket National Preserve established, including service as a volunteer director, officer, and president of the grass roots effort that led the nationwide "Save the Big Thicket" movement.

Most important, Howard has learned and loved the Big Thicket with a historian's perspective and a naturalist's point of view. He has studied it academically long enough to know how it came about and who its people were and how they used it. And he has walked it and poked around in it and loved it long enough to have a warm perception of it and a sympathy with it and with the life that moves in its woods and waters and grows from its soil. As a sensitive and professional writer, he communicates his knowledge and feeling for the Thicket with a deep understanding.

Howard is a good man to walk the river with — or Village Creek or the Big Thicket. We have walked it together.

> Francis Edward Abernethy
> Nacogdoches, Texas
> Autumn 1983

Dr. Abernethy is Executive Secretary/Editor of the Texas Folklore Society and the author of *Tales from the Big Thicket*. He is professor of English at Stephen F. Austin State University.

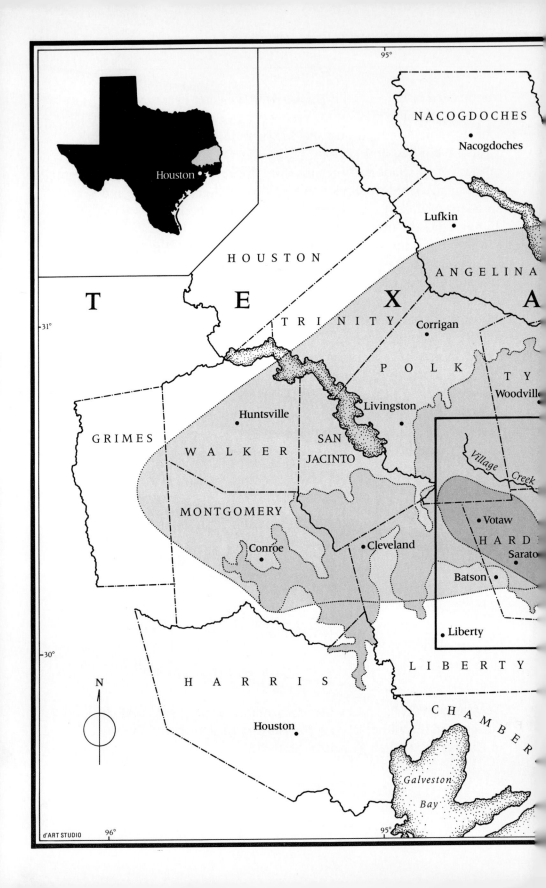

95°

NACOGDOCHES

Nacogdoches

Lufkin

HOUSTON

T   E   X   A

ANGELINA

31°

TRINITY

Corrigan

POLK

TY

Woodvill

Livingston

Huntsville

GRIMES

WALKER

SAN
JACINTO

Village   Creek

MONTGOMERY

Votaw

Conroe

Cleveland

HARD

Sarato

Batson

Liberty

30°

LIBERTY

N

HARRIS

CHAMBER

Houston

Galveston
Bay

96°

95°

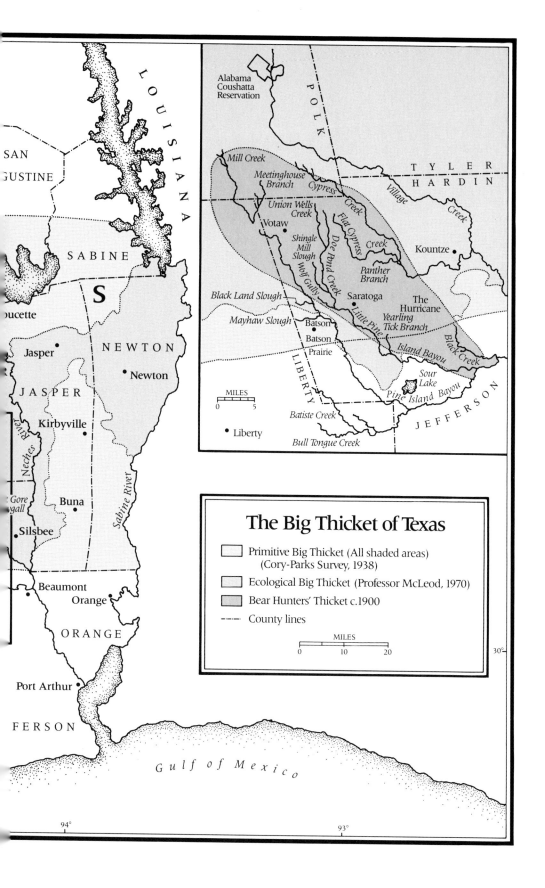

LOUISIANA

Alabama
Coushatta
Reservation

P O L K

SAN
GUSTINE

SABINE

S

T Y L E R

HARDIN

Mill Creek

Meetinghouse
Branch

Cypress

Village

Creek

Union Wells
Creek

Votaw

Flat Cypress

Creek

Kountze

Shingle
Mill
Slough

Doe Pond Creek

Panther
Branch

Wolf Gully

Black Land Slough

Saratoga

Little Pine

The
Hurricane
Yearling
Tick Branch

Mayhaw Slough

Batson

Island Bayou

Black Creek

oucette

NEWTON

Jasper

Batson
Prairie

L I B E R T Y

Sour
Lake

Newton

MILES

JASPER

0   5

Pine Island Bayou

J E F F E R S O N

Kirbyville

Neches River

Sabine River

Batiste Creek

Liberty

Bull Tongue Creek

Gore
ygall

Buna

Silsbee

Beaumont

Orange

The Big Thicket of Texas

Primitive Big Thicket (All shaded areas)
(Cory-Parks Survey, 1938)

Ecological Big Thicket (Professor McLeod, 1970)

Bear Hunters' Thicket c.1900

---·--- County lines

ORANGE

MILES

0   10   20

30°

Port Arthur

FERSON

Gulf of Mexico

94°   93°

Introduction

ONE DAY on a hike in late spring, I paused on a bluff over-looking Village Creek, a favorite waterway for canoeists and hikers in the Big Thicket of southeast Texas. I wanted to rest a moment and let the sounds and smells and sights of the reborn season sink into my head and, if they would, into my bones.

From where I stood, four distinct ecological systems, typical of four different parts of America, were within view; all I had to do was make slight turns. The Thicket embraces these varied natural complexes — a total of eight major ecosystems are found in the Big Thicket — more than any other point of North America, perhaps more than any other area of similar size in the world. This extreme diversity attracts scientists, artists, photographers, poets, and politicians from every state of the United States and many foreign lands.

In front of me was a field of cacti punctuated by Spanish bay-onet yucca banked up against a series of sand mounds. The scene was a picture postcard of the American southwestern desert.

To my right, perhaps a hundred yards away, loomed a dense, dark growth of trees hung with moss and rooted in muck. *Swamp* is the word most often used to describe the interior of such a place. Its dark water was dappled by light filtering through over-arching branches, now rippled by a turtle seeking a patch of sun on a fallen rotted stump sticking above water, now by a cotton-mouth moccasin seeking food. A better name for the place is *baygall.* It was formed in slow ecological steps from an open lake cut off from a nearby stream as the land shifted. At first grasses appeared on its borders, then shrubs, now trees. Debris patiently fills its depressions, creating turf that invites a whole new set of plants and animals. This scene could have been a cameo of Florida's and Georgia's famed Okefenokee.

To my left, large beech trees, stately loblolly pines, and lush southern magnolias rose above a spongy forest floor, open like a parkland. Several wild azaleas lifted the remnants of their fertilized blooms — a few weeks ago, those flowers had sent a fragrance, sweet and yet sharp, queenly and yet wild, throughout this grove. Squirrels scampered and quarreled across the scene. A dozen species of birds spoke. Anyone from Appalachia of eastern America would have felt at home here. These trees and shrubs and open forest floors are their own kind.

Behind me, a savannah sparkled with wild flowers and glistened green with new fronds of fern. Wild orchids bloom there amid carnivorous plants. The savannah is dominated by longleaf pines, the finest of the southern species of the genus *Pinus.* They had begun "candling," their branches putting forth long pale shoots shaped like elegant candles. Fountain sprays of needles shone in the sun. The scene struck me as another postcard picture — this one from the pinelands of the old South. The new South grows loblolly and slash pines; they get up, cut, and off to market fast, in twenty years or so. But the old South had lordly, slow-growing longleafs.

At my feet, a small purplish flower bent in a fresh breeze. It was an insignificant thing, low and pale. One's eye wanted to travel back to the picturesque Spanish bayonets or the shadowed baygall, or the beeches with their electric-green leaves, or the dazzle of the flowering savannah. The insignificant thing was *Polygala polygama,* commonly known as bitter milkwort or racemed milkwort. I carefully brushed away dirt from its base. Extending laterally from the base — but underground! — were more flowers. This peculiar plant produces flowers both above and below the surface. Why below? So that subterranean insects can perpetuate it by fertilization if the aboveground insects fail? Who knows such answers?

A deerscrape beneath a huge mockernut hickory tree caught my glance. Not far north of this spot, a panther had been seen a few days previously, crossing the Village Creek on a fallen log. Panthers were supposed to be long gone from the Thicket, as were bears. But the sighter was a person of knowledge and integrity; the panther had to be still surviving in these woods.

This creek was a corridor of legends. Gus Hooks had lived nearby. He was the world's fastest barefoot runner, they say. One day, on a bet, he raced a horse over a three-block course and got so far ahead that he turned around and finished the race running backward, beckoning the horse and its rider to hurry on! Another time, one midnight, old-timers allege he set the Hardin County courthouse on fire — his political faction wanted it moved anyway — and beat a posse to his house six miles away. When they thundered up on their lathered horses to his front yard, he appeared on the porch in his nightshirt, holding a lantern and innocently rubbing sleep from his eyes.

That spot of sandy bluff on the storied creek came to represent a lot of the Big Thicket to me. But one spot is just one spot. This book is about a lot of places in the Big Thicket: places in the woods, in the meadows, on the rivers and streams. And, yes, a few places in the imaginations of the Thicket's people.

Howard Peacock
Woodville, Texas

Contents

THE
BIG THICKET
OF TEXAS

CHAPTER 1

𝄢

Where Plants Eat Meat

PLANTS that eat meat are oddities everywhere and rarities in most places of the world. North America harbors five genera of carnivorous plants. Four of the five thrive in the Big Thicket. Now, however, some prankster has bought the missing one — a Venus's-flytrap — from a mail-order house and planted it beside a trail in a certain bog. It's doing quite well in its new home.

Almost everyone enjoys seeing carnivorous plants and understanding how they operate. The bladderwort sets underwater traps. Sundews and butterworts roll up their victims tortilla-fashion. Pitcher plants "drown" their prey in digestive juices.

The bladderwort (*Utricularia* is its scientific generic name) lowers baglike bladders below the surface of bogponds and then waits for curious bugs to paddle by. When a bug gets too close and brushes against special hairs sticking out from the bladder, a trapdoor flys open. This causes water to rush into the bladder, carrying the bug in with it. Once the meat is captured, the trapdoor closes. The bug is slowly digested. Then the trap is cocked again.

Sundews (*Drosera*) look like ruby-colored coins on the ground. Butterworts (*Pinguicula*) are innocent-looking plants with blue flowers on a six or eight-inch stem. Both trap bugs in sticky nectar on their leaves. A bug is attracted to aromatic nectar drops gleaming on a leaf. Its feet stick in the nectar. Slowly the leaf rolls up, something like a soft tortilla. The bug is then digested in chemicals excreted by the leaf.

3

The showiest plant among the meat-eaters is the pitcher plant. The species native to the Big Thicket is *Sarracenia alata*, popularly called the yellow pitcher plant. Rising between two and three feet tall, the plant has one leaf modified into a hooded tube. Many visitors liken it to a cobra with an extended hood. Bloodred veins thread through the tissue of the plant. Just under the hood, which may function to keep rain out of the tube, a collar exudes nectar that attracts insects, small frogs, and other creatures. Beguiled by the taste and fragrance, a small animal or bug slips into the tube and slides down its sides. When it tries to climb out, thousands of down-curving hairs on the inside of the tube frustrate its attempts, making escape difficult or impossible. Many victims tire and topple to the bottom, where digestive juices dissolve its meaty parts and leave the rest to stack up.

When people are mushing through a Big Thicket bog looking for meat-eating plants, all their senses are usually sharpened. They get curious about the neighboring plants and trees; for example, the sassafras.

The Big Thicket contains many tons of sassafras trees, and Thicket old-timers, to this day, make a delicious tea from the roots of the tree and claim it peps them up in the springtime. Root beer drinks are often flavored with the oil of sassafras, as are certain medicines and even some perfumes. And in the South, fish dishes are zinged up with dried leaves of sassafras, crumbled and called filé gumbo.

The sassafras is one of only two trees in North America that bear leaves with four different shapes. (The other is the mulberry.) The sassafras has a lance-shaped leaf, a three-fingered leaf, a right-hand "mitten," and a left-hand "mitten." Hikers in the Big Thicket woods are apt to pick a sassafras leaf and chew it to allay thirst.

Sassafras, which may live to be one thousand years old, grows north to Canada, but the Big Thicket is its natural southern limit.

Over three and a half centuries ago, in 1603, two ships sailed from England for the New World, their captains and crews commissioned to look for trees marked by unusual leaves. Pictures of these leaves had been drawn for them by botanical artists.

The ships' orders were to barter with the Indians for cutting rights, if necessary, and to load the vessels' holds with these trees, then make sail back to England as quickly as possible. For barter, the expedition had been stocked with "Hats of divers colours, Stockings and Shooes, Axes, Hookes, Sizzers, Bels, Beades, Bugles," and other useful and playful items.

The reputation of the sassafras stemmed from a publication called *Joyful Newes out of the Newe Founde Worlde,* written by no less a personage than the physician of Seville, Nicholas Monardes, and circulated in 1574. The distinguished doctor wrote that the sassafras was a "sovreign remedy for Quotidian Agewes [malaria], large importunate fevers . . . it comforteth the liver and the Stomacke, it dooeth maketh fatte, doth cause lust to meat . . . good for griefes of the breast caused of cold humours, griefes of the head, for them that bee lame and crepelles and them that not able to goe."

In those days, a London merchant could get rich with a shipload of sassafras because it was believed to cure many diseases. One could sell sassafras for 336 pounds sterling per ton. In dollars today, that's about $750, close to a fortune three centuries ago.

Another interesting plant often attracting the notice of Big Thicket hikers is the wahoo bush (*Euonymous americanus*), which prefers moist woods. "Wahoo" was the name given this shrub by the Indians. They found it growing in bogs and used its powdered inner bark as medicine. Perhaps its taste made the sick person gasp Wa-a-ahoo! Its fruits turn rosy-red in autumn, and that accounts for another of its names, strawberry bush. Folks in the Great Smoky Mountains, where it also grows, gave the plant its most striking name: heart's a bustin' with love.

In bogs can also be found the *Calopogon* orchid, one of many wild orchids bejeweling the Big Thicket. This species is also well known in New England and was a favorite of Thoreau's. In his *Journal* entry of July 7, 1852, he extols its radiant color, varying from pink to deep crimson, calls it a flower *par excellence,* and deplores its scientific label. "Calopogon!" he wrote. "They would blush still deeper if they knew the names man had given them. . . ."

5

Calopogon means "pretty beard," referring to the fringe on the bloom. The New England sage objected to the word *beard* being applied to such a delicate beauty.

In the Big Thicket, this orchid blooms in May. Its flowers have devised an ingenious technique for delivering pollen to bumble-bees. The grains of pollen are held on the tiny rods of a petal above the center of the flower. The Calopogon provides a landing strip for the bee immediately beneath the pollen. As the bee alights on the strip, a mechanism in the pollen perch is tripped, and the load is simply dumped on the bee's back. At the same time, the rods that dumped the load scrape the hairs on the bee's back, picking up golden grains from Calopogons previously visited, thereby carrying on the process of propagation.

When exploring a Big Thicket bog where the Calopogon and other orchids live, all four indigenous kinds of meat-eating plants may be found, but it doesn't happen often, and then only to the sharpest-eyed observer.

Two ancient plants, club moss (*Lycopodium* sp.) and royal fern (*Osmunda regalis*), can be often found in the same places where pitcher plants, sundews, and butterworts grow. Club moss has changed drastically since primitive times; now only inches high, it once grew as tall as trees, between 200 and 400 million years ago. Royal fern, however, appears today the same as it did 350 million years ago.

Students of evolution find certain Big Thicket bogs and seeps — areas in which underground water migrates to the surface of the land — of more than usual interest. Here, royal ferns, club mosses, orchids, and carnivorous plants grow side by side. These plant communities include very old kinds of plants and very young ones, for the orchids and meat-eaters only recently evolved upon the earth, perhaps less than 100 million years ago. All of these particular plants, primitive and recent alike, require a highly specialized environment, such as a moist area where the soil is low in nitrogenous matter. But the sole fact that they exist together, the ancient inhabitant and the newcomer, is worth noting in many student field journals.

6

These are just a few of the stories of the plants in the Big Thicket. The Big Thicket's legendary naturalist, Lance Rosier, estimated that one thousand or more flowering species can be found in the Thicket. Each one is a wonder in itself; each one has a unique story.

Where is the Big Thicket, the locale of all these rarities? And, more important, *what* is the Big Thicket?

CHAPTER 2

𝒦

Ecological Crossroads

ONE of the most remarkable things about the Big Thicket is its ecological variety. In this one area, originally covering 3.5 million acres but now reduced to less than a tenth of that size, there are eight different systems of nature — known as *plant associations* or *plant communities* — living side by side and intermingling with one another. It is the only such region in North America, and may be the only one of comparable size in the world.

Approximately one thousand kinds of flowering plants are found in the Big Thicket. Eighty-five species of trees tower over the landscape, including the American beech (*Fagus grandifolia*), which begins its natural range four thousand miles northward in Newfoundland and ends it in the Big Thicket. More than sixty species of wild shrubs, including the Piedmont azalea (*Rhododendron canescens*) and the silky camellia (*Stewartia malacodendron*). At least twenty kinds of wild orchids and twenty-six species of wild ferns, plus a staggering array of herbaceous plants and grasses and algae, fungi, mosses, and liverworts, all flourish here. Little wonder that the Thicket has been termed "America's Ecological Ark" and "The Biological Crossroads of North America."

The actual location of the Big Thicket is far from exact. Its boundaries remain in dispute. Some limit the Big Thicket to the "Bear Hunters' Thicket," a densely wooded area that covers Hardin County and southern Polk County, Texas. It was made famous by big-game hunts publicized in newspapers at the turn of the century. The little town of Saratoga, named after the sophisticated New York spa, was the center of the Bear Hunters' Thicket. Stories, legends, and lore of that locale still pass from generation to generation among the native families, who even today believe that this single small piece of southeast Texas is the true Big Thicket.

But scientists consider that the Big Thicket covers a much broader area.

To mark off the scientific boundaries, one may take a map and find Beaumont in the southeast corner of Texas near the Louisiana border. With a pencil, start at the northern edge of Beaumont and go due west to Interstate 45, between Houston and Conroe. Now head northwest to the little town of Roan's Prairie near the center of Grimes County. From that point, start slightly northeast, curving along the top of Lake Livingston, thence to Lufkin, and from there directly east to the Louisiana line at Toledo Bend Reservoir.

Roughly outlined, this is the classic biological Big Thicket. It covers a territory larger than the state of Connecticut. This is the area marked out in 1936 by the scientists V. L. Cory and H. B. Parks, who reported their findings — an astounding range of species in the plant and animal kingdoms — to the U.S. Biological Survey in Washington, D.C.

A more recent opinion on where the Big Thicket begins and ends is given by Professor Claude A. McLeod of Sam Houston University. He cites a particular type of forest, dominated by pines and mixed hardwoods, especially the beech tree (*Fagus grandifolia*), as defining the Big Thicket area. It covers about half the area of the Cory-Parks Survey.

Then there is a fourth definition given by the late *Houston Post* satirist, Hubert Mewhinney. He contended that the Big Thicket was located in people's heads, that it was more of an idea than an actual place.

Visitors often ask, "Is the Big Thicket the same thing as the Big Thicket National Preserve?"

The answer is no. The Big Thicket National Preserve is a collection of twelve representative pieces of the overall Thicket. It amounts to only 84,550 acres. The preserve was created by Congress and was signed into law on October 11, 1974, by President Gerald Ford. It is America's first natural sanctuary to be designated a preserve.

A preserve differs from a national park in basic purpose and usage. A park is dedicated to recreation and maximum use of facilities. A preserve is dedicated to the preservation of natural endowments — plant and animal life and their intermingling and evolution, to which humans may be witnesses. Most, if not all, of the major ecosystems found in the Big Thicket region are represented in the dozen geographical Units of the National Preserve. The National Park Service administers the development and public use of the preserve. The units range in size from the 550 acres of the Loblolly Unit to 25,024 acres in the Lance Rosier Unit.

While its boundaries remain a matter of opinion, the real question is: *What* is the Big Thicket? And answers to that question are even more varied than the ideas about its exact location.

First, the Big Thicket is a special place of nature. Where plant life is so rich, animal life also proliferates. Animals, after all, need to eat, and the food chain for all creatures, including humans, begins with plants. Only plants can take energy from the sun and convert it — a process known as "photosynthesis" — into a form that animals can use for themselves and pass on to other animals.

In addition to mammals, reptiles, fishes, amphibians, insects, and other classes of animals, more species of birds live in or migrate into the Big Thicket than are found in many entire states of the United States or in many other nations. About 350 species of birds fly the Big Thicket. Among them are several rare and endangered species: Bachman's warbler, the brown-headed nuthatch, the red-cockaded woodpecker; and, some say, even the gigantic ivory-billed woodpecker, which has a wingspan of almost two feet. This woodpecker is believed by many bird authorities to be extinct, to have disappeared entirely from the earth. If any ivorybills still live — the last official sightings having come in the

1970s — they might well have taken a last refuge in the depths of the Big Thicket.

The Big Thicket is home for so many kinds of creatures because its plant communities provide a tremendous variety of food, fulfilling the needs of microscopic bacteria as well as ten-foot-long alligators.

A plant community is a society of certain plants that live harmoniously with their own kind and with certain animals that may help propagate the plants through pollenation or by spreading seed. Both plants and animals thrive in particular combinations of soil, water, air, and weather conditions. When foreign or strange species of plants intrude into a successful plant community, they may find its conditions either hospitable or hostile — even deadly. For example, a swamp would be lethal to a species of cactus constructed to live in the desert. But some intruders are able to make themselves at home in almost any environment, adapting to new circumstances and new plant and animal neighbors, perhaps in time evolving into altogether new species.

These are the eight major plant communities, or ecosystems, identified to date in the Big Thicket:

Palmetto-Hardwood Flats. Here, palmettos fan watery swamps beneath tall bald cypresses, water tupelos, and willow oaks, the trees often draped in Spanish moss. This is a favorite haunt of water moccasins, one of the four genera of poisonous snakes found in the Big Thicket. Palmettos once grew high enough to shade a man on a horse, but few today measure over six feet tall. The big ones were cut years ago.

Prairie. Tall grasses found on the plains of the United States all the way to Canada, and other grasses and flowers native to the coastal prairies of the Gulf Coast, feature this open ecosystem.

Stream Floodplain. These areas are similar to the Palmetto-Hardwood Flats, but are terraced. Their high ridges support sweet gums and oaks that don't care for constantly wet feet, also swamp maple and ironwood in large numbers. The low areas flood each year. This plant association is locally famous for its titi ("tight-eye") thickets, which are often impenetrable.

Longleaf Pine Uplands. These are hilly, well-drained areas dominated by the stately longleaf pine.

Pine Savannah Wetlands. Home of meat-eating pitcher plants, sundews, and butterworts; a dozen showy wild orchid species, including the Calopogon; finicky Arkansas blueberry and staggerbush, which both wage chemical warfare on the plants they don't like: primitive club moss and lush ferns. Loblolly and longleaf pines thrive in this soggy terrain. The areas are noted for lush displays of springtime wild flowers.

Arid Sandylands. Cactus, yucca, and sandhills, representative of a southwestern desert, characterize this dry landscape, a striking departure from the swamps and dense forests that typify southeast Texas for many people.

Acidbog-Baygall. Wet the year around, a baygall is a low place, often a pond or lake, marked by decaying plants that cause extremely high acidity in the water. Trees frequently topple into the muck because their roots weaken in water. Acid-loving plants, including the carnivorous bladderwort, thrive here. The name baygall derives from the sweetbay magnolia and the gallberry holly, two especially abundant species.

Beech-Magnolia-Loblolly. This is the most impressive of all the plant communities in the Thicket, found in hilly areas creased by running creeks. Huge specimens of beech, magnolia, loblolly pine, sugar maple, and white oak tower over wild azaleas, jack-in-the-pulpit, hearts a bustin' with love bushes, and hundreds of other kinds of wild shrubs and plants that live close to the forest floor. This plant association is considered by some scientists to be the climax ecosystem of the Thicket, meaning that it eventually will dominate or eliminate the other plant communities in its territory if human activities do not interfere with nature's processes.

These various plant associations have been identified by Geraldine Watson of Silsbee, Texas, who combines scientific training with more than forty years of astute and artistic observation of the land, plants, animals, and humans occupying the Big Thicket. She was born in the Thicket and has been a lifelong student of its changes and characteristics. Her booklet, *Big Thicket Plant Ecol-*

12

ogy: An Introduction (Big Thicket Museum Publication Series Number 5, Saratoga, Texas, 1975), is considered basic to an understanding of the Thicket's environment. Other Big Thicket scientists — Dr. Paul Harcombe of Rice University, Dr. Peter Marks of Cornell, and Indian taxonomist Geyata Ajilvsgi — acknowledge Watson's expertise while offering different approaches.

The Big Thicket, then, is a virtual paradise for anyone who enjoys nature. It fascinates scientists, who come from various parts of the world to study the interplay of ecosystems. It inspires artists, journalists, poets, and photographers. It has become a favorite refuge for anyone in southeast Texas who gets the urge to take off for the woods.

But the Big Thicket sometimes disappoints visitors, too. "Why, it just looks like plain old woods to me," some say. "Where are the wild orchids? We've driven for miles and never saw a single orchid!"

People who like instant panoramas while whizzing through on a hurry-up vacation usually don't think too highly of the Thicket. One tourist complained that she expected to drive up to an opening in the woods, sit in her car, and see wild orchids and brilliant parrots decorating the "jungle." Then she could get on her way to the Astroworld in Houston.

The truth of the matter is, any visitor needs a curious eye, stamina, and a patient heart to appreciate the Big Thicket. Most of the original primitive wilderness has given way to towns, roads, farms, ranches, and the other spoor of civilization. Only a small bit of the original Thicket has been saved, and that bit is broken into scattered fragments. Breathtaking sights remain, but one must seek them out. They don't rise up and smite a visitor like the Grand Tetons.

The power and appeal of the Big Thicket is subtle, much like the wit of many of its native people. One learns to enjoy the small along with the gigantic. A visitor can marvel at the exquisitely designed seedbox of a weedy *Ludwigia* as much as at the sweep of a climax forest dominated by huge beeches, magnolias, and loblolly pines, or at the splendor of a sylvan ravine flowing with wild azaleas. One may stop to turn over a green leaf with white markings — is it a crippled crane-fly orchid or simply common sweetbriar? Ah! The rich purple underside reveals it as the orchid, *Tipularia*.

But before plants and animals filled the woods, before men's feet pressed down the first crude path, before anything happened to make the Thicket ecologically unique, the ground itself had to be established; soil — rock and clay and loamy silt — had to be laid down and shaped by the waters.

CHAPTER 3

🦅

Laying Down the Land

THE CREATION of Big Thicket land began millions of years ago in the far north of the American continent. Immense glaciers formed across the northeastern United States and Canada, using waters from the world's oceans for their icy expansion and causing sea levels gradually to sink. Originally, waters of the Gulf of Mexico covered the Big Thicket area. When the gulf's waters receded because of the formation of the glaciers in the north, the land was gradually exposed. The retreating waters deposited silt and soil as they flowed south.

At least four times the glaciers formed and melted, and each time the land of the future Big Thicket was exposed, then covered, and constantly reshaped as the Gulf of Mexico retreated and advanced. Geologists say that most of the land of the Big Thicket was deposited in the periods between the melting of one glaciation and the formation of the next one. This took place during the Pleistocene epoch, which began 2 million to 2.5 million years ago. About 10,000 years ago that epoch closed.

Strange animals ranged the Big Thicket in Pleistocene times, including the tapir, capybara, mammoth, and mastodon. The mammoth grew up to thirteen feet tall at the shoulder, had long curved tusks, and kept its elephantlike body warm with a hairy hide. The mastodon of the Big Thicket was also a huge, hairy elephant, but lacked curved tusks. Other prehistoric Thicket dwellers survived to become familiar today: the wild horse, deer, opossum, and bear.

When the glacial turbulence of the Pleistocene epoch ended, the Big Thicket region contained five major geologic formations. A geologic formation is a body or grouping of rocks that are so alike that they form a distinctive unit. The oldest, perhaps more than twelve million years in age, is called the Fleming Formation, which existed prior to the Pleistocene epoch, and is located north of Woodville in the vicinity of Lufkin. It is marked by lime-filled clay and sandstone.

Next oldest is the Willis Formation, perhaps two million to three million years in age, found on a line from Livingston east to Woodville, Jasper, and Newton. It remains one of the most popular areas in Texas for collectors of petrified wood.

Layered on the downward slant of Big Thicket land toward the Gulf of Mexico are increasingly younger geologic formations: the Bentley, deposited several hundred thousand years ago; the Montgomery, about 100,000 years old; and the Beaumont, say 70,000 years in age. Younger still are the Deweyville Terrace, 12,000 to 34,000 years in age, whose deposits lie along the Neches and Trinity rivers; and the Holocene Alluvium, probably less than 5,000 years old.

Today, there are many different kinds of soils in the Big Thicket: more than fifty basic mixtures of sand, loam, clay, and rock that make fertile beds for the vast numbers of different trees, shrubs, forbs, flowers, fungi, and algae.

This plant life, taking root in soils whose origins hark back to the Pleistocene glaciers, attracted food-seeking animals. Those hungry creatures in turn attracted human hunters seeking nuts, berries, and meat — chiefly meat. Using crude but effective weapons, these earliest hunters tracked the white-tailed deer and black bear into the shadows of the green virginal wilderness. They knew how to find and fetch meat in any terrain. They were Indians.

16

CHAPTER 4

𝕂

Hunting Parties
and War Paint

ALL THROUGH THE LAND that was one day to be called
Texas, Indians roamed, hunted, and made war. Fierce Apaches
ruled the deserts and the awesome mountains of West Texas. The
world's greatest horse warriors, the Comanches, rode the plains
of the north, and the central hills. On the Gulf Coast were giants
of aboriginal America, the Karankawas, so strong that they hunted
with bows six feet tall. Other tribes famed in the annals of the
Texas frontier were the Lipans, Tonkawas, Wichitas, and Kiowas.

In the east, four tribes penetrated the wilderness known today
as the Big Thicket. They were the Atakapan, the Caddo, and the
Alabama and Coushatta. Today the Alabama and Coushatta tribes,
retaining separate languages but living together, remain.

Atakapan is an Indian word meaning "man-eater." Some of
these Indians were known among early Texas travelers and settlers to be cannibals — cooking and eating enemies killed in battle
or captured. A typical Atakapan male had a short, thick body,
large head, unusually large ears and mouth, and a big nose. His
teeth were stained from chewing leaves containing tannin and
dyes. Tattoos marched across his body, discoloring his swarthy
skin. His hair was coarse and usually matted with dirt.

Various groups of Atakapans lived along the southern and
western fringes of the Big Thicket. Harvesting the open marshes
and prairies between the Thicket and the Gulf of Mexico, they
subsisted mainly on fish, water lotus, shrimps, crabs, and birds'

THE BIG THICKET OF TEXAS

eggs. During the winter months, the men ventured into the Big Thicket to hunt deer, bear, and smaller animals. They also traveled to the plains west of their home grounds to hunt bison. (The shaggy animal of the plains is sometimes called a "buffalo," but that name should be reserved for an animal native to Africa and Asia.) Frequently, however, the Atakapans ran into the hunting and war parties of other tribes on the plains.

An Atakapan brave who brought home a bison skin often made it into a robe with mystical designs painted on the inside. The brave wore his robe during the winter as a badge of prestige, as well as to keep warm. He went barefooted during the freezing winter and summer alike. A simple breechcloth was often his only other article of clothing.

His Atakapan mate wore an animal skin cut into a circle with a hole at the center. She dropped the garment over her head and tied the waist with thin strips of hide.

To trust the Atakapans was risky, according to European explorers like the Frenchman Simars de Bellisle, who lived with the Indians from 1719 to 1721. In the wars between the Spanish and French, the Indians acted as double agents, spying for both sides and even selling firearms to both. However, they also encouraged peace rather than conflict among Indian tribes, helping bring about an alliance between the Lipan Apaches and the Caddoes, who had been ancient enemies.

The members of the Atakapan tribes were never very numerous. They had come in small numbers from southwestern Louisiana into southeastern Texas, only to have their scant population riddled by war and disease, almost to the point of extinction. French and Spanish efforts to "civilize" them never succeeded. They have faded into history.

At the opposite end of the Big Thicket, on the north, lived the Caddoes. Judging by the difference between their way of life and that of the Atakapans, it might have been the opposite end of the world. The Caddoes were among the most cultured and advanced Indian tribes. Today they are admired by students of American

18

Indian societies for their accomplishments in agriculture, art, and other practices of a progressive people.

Living in the fertile valleys on the northern rim of the Big Thicket, the Caddoes were expert farmers, as well as good hunters and skilled fighters. Using the shoulder blade of the bison as their only farming tool, they raised abundant crops of corn, beans, squash, sunflower seed, and tobacco. Unlike the many tribes that lived on a feast-or-famine basis, the Caddoes provided for future needs; they always kept a two-year supply of seed corn.

Anybody today who goes trotline fishing uses the same methods developed by the Caddoes. A long thick rope, strung from one creek bank to a bank opposite, was tied with a series of short lines every few feet. The short lines were baited on bone hooks, then dropped into the creek.

Deadly hunters, Caddo men were trained to camouflage themselves with a deerskin and antlers, so that they not only were able to sneak up on a fidgety buck or doe, but also could actually attract the animal closer for the kill. In the Big Thicket, Caddoes also hunted black bear, wild turkey, and duck. They used the bear grease and a vermilion pigment to decorate their bodies for war.

War either was a means of revenge or was used simply to enhance a brave's reputation as a warrior. Caddoes took scalps and tanned them as permanent trophies of victory.

Their efficiency in farming, fighting, hunting, and fishing gave them time to develop arts and sports. Caddo pottery and baskets are still highly prized for their beauty and utility. Their deerskin clothes — shiny black, and decorated with white seeds — were admired wherever they went. The clothing's unique deep luster was achieved by tanning the skin with bison and deer brains. The Caddoes created music with flutes made from bird bones and reeds, rattles made from gourds, and two sets of drums — one fashioned from hollow logs, the other, from jars that had hides stretched and tied over their mouths after being partially filled with water.

If one were to spend a typical day in a Caddo camp, here are some of the activities that might be witnessed:

○ A doctor treating a sick man by making him sweat. The patient lies on a platform over a bed of hot coals. The doctor makes motions as if he is drawing worms from the man; that element of the treatment is ritualistic. If a doctor fails too often to cure his patients, he may be killed.

○ A woman being tattooed with plant and animal symbols. Her skin is pricked with needles made from small bones. Powdered charcoal is then rubbed into the scored skin. Both men and women tattoo their faces and bodies.

○ A baby whose head is being gently but firmly tapered toward the top. The Caddoes were naturally handsome people, according to the European explorers, but believed in deforming their heads for ritualistic reasons. The young mother of a child performed the birthing herself. In Caddo tradition, she chose a spot beside a river and built a small hut. She sank a center pole to grasp during childbirth. When time came for the baby to arrive, she went into the hut and gave birth. She then bathed herself and the baby in the river (no matter if the weather was freezing) and returned promptly to her duties in the village.

○ A house-raising. The atmosphere of this project is more like that of a party than work. When one of the tribe's families needs a new home, they notify the chief, or caddi. A date is then set for the construction. Tammas, or subchiefs, are appointed to supervise the work. They, in turn, appoint the workers and assign them specific jobs, such as who will bring the poles, who will be the pole-fasteners, who will bring the thick grass for covering the house, and so on. The night before the house-raising, the Tammas sleep at the site. At dawn, they summon the work party. If a man reports late, he gets switched on his bare chest by his Tamma, while his friends hoot in laughter. If a woman is late to the job, she gets switched on her shoulders as her friends giggle. The work goes quickly and happily. Meanwhile, the family that will live in the house is cooking up a storm. In early afternoon when the new home is finished, they will serve a heaping feast to all who have helped: venison, wild turkey, corn, pecans, plums, cherries, grapes, and tender roots and tubers.

o Boys competing in games of footracing, hockey, and pole-and-hoop, the latter testing their abilities in throwing a pole through a rolling hoop.

o A group of boys being shown how to use weapons of war. The teachers are their uncles, their mothers' brothers. Caddo custom held those men to be the most important male relatives.

o A group of boys and girls clustering around a wrinkled Indian woman. Grandmothers had the duty of teaching Caddo children right behavior.

A typical day in camp would be full and fascinating, for the Caddo people were energetic, highly accomplished, and often unpredictable. They were famous for their hospitality and just as famous for their cruelty.

The Caddoes entered European recorded history in 1541, when they attacked a Spanish scouting party led by the colorful explorer Hernando de Soto. The attackers were descended from people who had probably come in boats over the Gulf of Mexico from the Caribbean, centuries earlier, landing at an unknown place or places on the Gulf Coast of Texas. Gradually the Caddoes migrated north and east — hundreds of miles north and all the way to the Atlantic coast.

These Indian peoples were known to white scholars as Mound Builders. They built earthen mounds, quite similar to the stone mounds of the Aztecs, Toltecs, and Mayas. These structures varied greatly in size, but usually had a square or rectangular shape and a flat top. A stairway ascended on at least one side of the mound. Temple mounds were used for religious ceremonies. A fire built in the center of the temple was not allowed to die. It was fed with four large logs pointed north, south, east, west.

France and Spain fought over Caddo land for two hundred

years. The French withdrew as a force in Texas history after the Louisiana Purchase in 1803. That transaction, in which the United States paid France $15 million, virtually doubled the size of the nation.

The name "Texas" comes from a Caddo word meaning "ally" or "friend." The Caddo word sounded like "tayshas." Spaniards picked it up and slightly changed the pronunciation.

Of all their dramatic traits, probably the most striking was the Caddo habit of greeting strangers with loud wailing and tears. Even if the Indians felt friendly toward visitors, eardrum-shattering sounds of weeping came from both men and women. If a decision was made to kill intruders, however, only the women wept. French and Spanish adventurers in Caddo country soon learned to watch for this alarming and telling sign.

By 1770, this great Indian people had almost disappeared. Caddo women had intermarried with traveling French traders, changing the tribal bloodline, which was traced through women. Caddo lands were occupied by both French and Spanish forces vying for power in Texas. Epidemic diseases ravaged their villages. By 1855, most of the remaining Caddoes — no more than several hundred — were living on the Brazos Indian Reservation in north central Texas. In 1859, an organization of white settlers greedy for all Indian lands planned a campaign to massacre every Indian in the state. The supervisor of the reservation, Robert S. Neighbors, saved about three hundred Caddoes by taking them on a secret march to Oklahoma. Neighbors was killed by the whites planning the massacre for sparing these Caddoes. Very little was heard of the Caddoes afterward. But in their primacy, the Caddoes were the most numerous, creative, and progressive of all the tribes in Texas. Most remaining members of the tribe now live in Oklahoma.

As the Caddoes slowly vanished, another Indian people, the Alabama and Coushatta tribes who lived and traveled together, appeared in the northern reaches of the Big Thicket. They came from the southeastern part of the United States. The first of these two tribes had given its name to the southern state of Alabama.

22

Unlike other Indians of the Big Thicket — the Atakapans and the Caddoes — the Alabama-Coushatta tribes who arrived in Texas in the late 1700's chose to be patient and cooperative in their relations with the Texas authorities, but they had proved their mettle as warriors. When the Texas colonists were fighting Spain for Texas soil in 1813, a company of only twenty-five Coushatta braves sympathetic to the colonists charged a line of twenty-five hundred Spanish regulars and militia. Apart from a few battles, however, these Indians chose peace as their way of dealing with the authorities.

The Alabama and Coushatta people are kin to the Creek and Chickasaw tribes. The Alabamas first appear in European history in the same way as the Caddoes: Hernando de Soto, the Spanish explorer, attacked a village of "Alibamo" Indians, as they were called, in 1541. (That was the year his soldiers also encountered the Caddoes in a pitched battle.) At that time the Alabamas were living in northeastern Mississippi. They migrated eastward during the next two hundred years, settling on the Alabama River. Then joined by the Coushattas, they gradually split into four groups. One remained on the Coosa River in Alabama; one established villages in Louisiana; a third group headed west to Oklahoma; the fourth came to the Big Thicket. Their movement was piece-meal, occurring over a period of about sixty years.

While the Alabamas settled three villages on the Neches River in the upper Thicket, the Coushattas continued about sixty miles west to the Trinity River, where four hundred of them established three villages: Colita's Village, Battise Village, and Long King's Village.

Trouble quickly followed. The Texas war of independence from Mexico erupted in the fall of 1835. The Coushattas had been active allies of the Texas colonists for years — blazing the "Coushatta Trace" through two hundred fifty miles of wilderness from the Sabine River boundary between Texas and Louisiana to the settlement of La Bahia, now the town of Goliad, and serving as scouts and sentinels for the Texans. But their loyal service went unrewarded. The Alabamas fared no better in their dealings with

23

the Texans. Just before the Battle of San Jacinto, where Texas won its independence, a few Alabamas went back to Louisiana for a short time, but the majority of them remained in their villages and fed the Texas colonists fleeing before the army of General Santa Anna, president of Mexico and victor at the Alamo.

Sam Houston, an American hero and a legend in Texas, became a champion for the Alabama Indians. He was one of the best white friends the Indians of Texas ever had. His leadership in relieving the plight of the homeless Alabamas and Coushattas, whose lands often had been taken from them in claims by white settlers, as well as other tribes in Texas, resulted in 1,110 acres of the Big Thicket being purchased by the state of Texas in 1854 from various private landowners for a reservation. The price was two dollars per acre. Seventy-four years later, in 1928, the United States government added 3,071 acres, also purchased from individual owners. Today, about five hundred Indians live on the Alabama-Coushatta Reservation. For many years it was the only Indian reservation in the entire state of Texas, a land once famed for its many Indian tribes.

Tradition states that every member of these two tribes belonged to one of twelve clans: Alligator, Bear, Beaver, Bird, Daddy Longlegs, Deer, Panther, Wildcat, Wind, Salt, Turkey, and Wolf. The Alabama and Coushatta peoples felt a strong kinship with nature. They made medicines from leaves, barks, roots, and flowers. The elements of water, fire, earth, and air furnished a basis for their religious teachings and legends.

Young members of the tribes were taught that one of the strongest principles of the Alabama-Coushatta family was community action. Everyone helped dig water wells, cut wood for the church and the school stoves, and harvest community crops. They all joined in tribal dances, games, and sports; everything was done with a spirit of unity. Almost everyone participated.

Today, thousands of visitors are welcomed each year to the Alabama-Coushatta Reservation. Dancers perform in colorful costumes to exciting drumbeats; a splendid historical pageant-drama,

24

Beyond the Sundown, is presented on summer evenings in a fine outdoor theater; and one of the most beautiful forests of the Big Thicket can be explored with Indian guides.

There, among the giant trees, it is easy to wonder how it felt to be an Indian in the days before the white man's wagons came rumbling across the rivers and into the Big Thicket.

CHAPTER 5

Across the Mighty Waters

HEADING WEST! By the early nineteenth century, this was the spirit of the times, the magic message. America was ready to stretch its horizons.

Settlers came to the Big Thicket floating their tough pioneer wagons across the Mississippi and Sabine and Neches rivers, and maybe the Atchafalaya, too. *HOO-O-O-O-AH-H-H-H-H!* You can almost hear the echoing holler even now.

The first settlers in the Big Thicket came in the 1820s. They avoided the Thicket itself — the deep woods and shadowy swamps were too forbidding. They took up land on the fringes, leaving the forests to fugitive horse thieves, outlaws, and other characters who needed a hiding place where they would be neither followed nor traced. The Thicket became that kind of haven.

Families that crossed the big rivers in the 1830s were more determined than those who had arrived ten years earlier and had stayed on the fringes. The second wave of settlers didn't hesitate to move into the uncharted interior of the Thicket to make their homes. They came mostly from southern states to the east — Tennessee (Davy Crockett and other heroes at the Alamo came from there), Georgia, Alabama, Mississippi, Arkansas, and Louisiana. Settlers came from many other states in the new American nation as well. All of them had an adventuring spirit. Just about all of them dreamed of making a better life for themselves in Texas.

That day didn't come quickly for most families. After the long and dangerous trip, they had to find a piece of land they liked and make sure it wasn't already taken by someone who might have gotten there earlier. But in those days, settlers usually had their pick of the land.

A newly arrived family camped under trees while a log cabin was built. The cabin was made from pine logs laid on top of one another, notched at the ends to fit snugly. Spaces between the logs were chinked with red clay. The most important part of the structure was the fireplace. It was made of mud or clay strengthened with sticks and straw, stoutly framed with poles cut from the nearby woods. Tapered toward the top, the fireplace drew smoke upward. Fireplaces furnished warmth, light, and served as the cooking area. Also very important was the roof, for the Big Thicket was often pounded with heavy rains and swept by wild winds. Housetops were shingled with boards, usually split from a tree called the swamp chestnut oak. Some people called it the basket oak tree because it made good baskets, too.

Each family cleared a spot in the Thicket woods big enough to plough and to work with one horse. That spot would grow sufficient corn, peas, and sweet potatoes for the household. Some families also had grapevines. Sugarcane was planted to give the kids — and the old folks, too — a treat.

By the time a boy was twelve years old, he was helping the father of the family provide meat. He had been taught to hunt wild turkey, rabbit, possum, birds, deer, and the wild hogs that roamed the Thicket. Many boys, in their learning days, got chased up a tree by an old "tush hog" — the boss hog of a wild pack. Its long tusks, or tushes, were like eight-inch swords, curving from the corners of its mouth; it knew how to maim and even kill with them. Moreover, a typical tush hog had a furious temper.

A boy of ten or twelve learned how to work with horses and oxen. His father taught him how to use an ax and the other simple but versatile tools of a homestead farm in the wilderness. He learned how to use his hands and muscles to produce food. In the woods, he learned how to use his head, for the Big Thicket

27

could be a threatening place. It harbored dangerous animals and jungle-thick places where directions became confused, places where even experienced woodsmen got lost.

When a girl reached the age of ten or twelve, she was already an important member of the household. She worked with her mother cooking, making cloth and clothes, gardening, and nursing those who were sick and hurt. Her domain was the house and its immediate surroundings.

Because there was so much to do just to stay alive and well and make a little progress, the division of labor was clear-cut. Except for very young children, everyone in the family had specific jobs to do.

Children went to school in the wintertime when they weren't needed to help in the family's work. That is, they went to school if there was someone in their territory who knew how to teach and who had offered to be a teacher. As often as not, someone's house served as the school. Many schools were located simply under a well-known tree. The town of Liberty was one of the very few places in the Thicket that prided itself on a real one-room school. The room could hold up to fifty students. When the people of Liberty wanted a teacher, they put an ad in the newspaper. The desired qualifications were "sobriety and attention to business."

A student's seat in a Thicket school was apt to be a spot on a pine plank laid across a couple of barrels or nail kegs. A school desk was of similar construction, except higher. Girls and boys of all ages studied reading, writing, and numbers. Books were few. Many children learned to read using the Bible as their textbook, for if any family owned a book, it was most likely the Bible.

Children's clothes were made of cloth spun from cotton or wool. Women made sure to bring their spinning wheels when the wagon was loaded for the family's long trip to Texas and the Big Thicket. They sacrificed other beloved pieces of furniture for the spinning wheel. After they had spun thread from raw cotton or wool, they made a long single piece of cloth on a simple loom. From that piece, clothes for the entire family were cut and hand

28

sewn. A mother or daughter with a flair for design could put a little style into the cuts, but usually there wasn't much time for such fancifying.

Children went barefooted most of the time, and always during the summer. Their feet got so tough that they could walk almost anywhere without discomfort. A story of the time concerned a boy who stood on a piece of red-hot iron in his father's blacksmith shop and got severely burned before he knew anything was wrong.

When shoes were a necessity, fathers would buy or trade for a whole cowhide. Feet would be measured and marked while children stood on the hide. After cutting the outlines from the hide, a father used a simple shoe last to fashion the shoes. Leather thongs were used for lacings. If the shoes weren't comfortable for tough-skinned feet, mothers might weave a pair of soft wool socks for a birthday or Christmas gift.

Good times came, too, breaking up the pattern of work in the wilderness. One such time was a logrolling. Children loved to hear that a neighbor was planning to clear some land. That meant a holiday, a good time for everybody, was in store. From miles around, friends traveled by horse and wagon, even on foot, to join in the logrolling day.

While the women and girls made quilts and cooked huge amounts of game and vegetables, wild-fruit pies and whole-grain breads, the men and boys cleared space for new crops. Trees were felled and logs rolled away; they would be used later for a building project. Underbrush was burned, great care being taken that the fire was contained within bounds. Hours later, the space would be clear and clean, ready for the owner's plough. Feasting would follow, then games and dancing. More often than not, one of the neighbors could fiddle. Boys learned to "call" the dancers to the fiddler's tunes. If neighbors were natives of Louisiana, they might even dance a quadrille, a French dance involving four couples. Young people who weren't dancing, watching the dances, or calling for the fiddler often played dominoes. And there was usually an expert storyteller among the older neighbors. Yarns spun at logrollings were transmitted from generation to generation, carrying history, legend, and tradition forward by the spoken word.

Young people whose families came to the logrolling in wagons had a fine ride home. Blending with the creak of the wheels, the rhythmic clopping of horses' hooves, and the sounds and smells of dark woods, rising tall at the sides of the wagon lane, were memories of fun, friends, and heaping plates of food. Sleep would soon come, stealing over tired muscles relaxing in deep layers of fresh hay.

Gradually, each family tamed its piece of the Thicket wilderness. It took work by every member of a family to make a homestead a home. Life was hard, but for the most part, good. The settlers lived and worked in the open air, amid superb natural beauty, with more kinds of nature's creatures than they could count for company. More people arrived and settled in. Neighbors' cabins got closer and closer. With the people came stores. Eventually, men with big saws came to the Thicket woods and gazed at the sky-punching pine trees that they knew would make some of the world's finest lumber. Those men made history, but it was not always the kind of history a person likes to know about. Much of it was brutal and ugly. For a long time, the Big Thicket trembled as its giant trees were quivered and toppled by axes and the big saws. It became a wounded wilderness.

CHAPTER 6

The Sustained Assault

VIRGIN FORESTS covering about three million acres of the Big Thicket, forests created and nurtured by nature over centuries, were leveled in only six decades.

It started in the 1850s, when the thick forests of the Great Lakes region had been lumbered almost to exhaustion. Commercial timber interests in the northern and midwestern cities of the country looked for new sources of wood. The yellow pine of the Big Thicket — "yellow" pine meant either longleaf, loblolly, or shortleaf — took their fancy. They made arrangements to buy it up.

Until then, the only reason to cut down trees in the Big Thicket had been to build a cabin or barn, or to clear a piece of land for a garden or family crops.

About 1860, the Big Thicket began furnishing lumber in small quantities to northern markets. Transportation was still primitive, so the logs were floated down the Sabine River to Orange and down the Neches River to Beaumont. There, sawmills cut the logs into boards for loading onto ships or trains bound north.

That trade ended abruptly when the Civil War erupted. Texas threw its support to the Confederacy over the protests of General Sam Houston, who argued that the young union of states must be preserved. Some Big Thicket settlers formed companies to fight for the Confederacy, but more than a few pioneers refused to join any army at all. They wanted to be left alone by any and all governments, and took refuge in the deep woods where Confederate search teams couldn't track them.

After the war, soldiers returned home to the Thicket, and families began rebuilding their lives from scratch. But by the early 1870s, the critical need for new lumber in the war-wrecked nation once again focused attention on the giant pines and lush hardwoods of the Big Thicket.

Construction of the Houston and Great Northern Railroad in 1872 signaled the start of massive cutting in the forests. Unlike any previous transportation system, this railroad was capable of hauling thousands of tons of logs daily from the Thicket to the cities.

Four more railroads followed the Houston and Great Northern — the Houston East and West Texas Railroad, the Sabine and East Texas, the Trinity and Sabine Railroad, and the world-renowned Santa Fe.

Later came the Texas and New Orleans Railroad, which eventually became part of the continent-spanning Southern Pacific system. That was followed by the Saint Louis and Southwestern Railroad, the Beaumont and Great Northern, and the Orange and Southwestern.

Main-line tracks and branch lines sliced through almost every dry league of land in the Big Thicket. Empty boxcars disappeared into the woods, then came clacking out piled high with sap-streaming logs. The process was repeated every daylight hour, seven days a week, year after year.

In addition to the major railroads above, many of the large lumber mills built their own railroads to serve the areas in which they were felling timber. Small tramlines — short distances of track connecting cutting areas with the main line — also criss-crossed the Thicket.

During the Reconstruction following the Civil War, much of the nation's rebuilding was accomplished with lumber sawed from Big Thicket pines and hardwoods.

The lumber barons of east Texas — a relatively few men who bought the forest lands cheaply or leased cutting rights for even

32

less, who owned the sawmills, and who sold the finished product to national markets — gave little thought to replacing the trees they felled. The prevailing mentality of the times was to cut, saw, sell, and then bank the huge profits. Many hillsides and valleys were stripped of mature trees and saplings, gouged by the log-hauling process, then abandoned, littered with debris.

The sawmill town was a direct result of the years of steady timbering. Throughout the Big Thicket area, sawmills had sprouted up to slice the logs brought from the cutting sites. A sawmill soon spawned shanties and shacks for workers, then a store. Next might come a church, then a school.

Wage earning in a sawmill town was a new kind of life for the descendants of pioneers and backwoodsmen. Living space was cramped. Men worked long and dangerous hours at whirling saws. Women, concerned with bearing families, persisted in establishing civilizing influences, such as schools and houses of worship. Children worked too, and attended school when they weren't needed for chores; and they somehow managed to find time for games and practical jokes, like youngsters of most times and most places.

CHAPTER 7

𝐊

*Growing Up
in a Sawmill Town*

IN THE WOODS, find a pine sapling about twelve or fifteen feet tall and about six inches wide at the base. Climb on a friend's shoulders and grasp the top portion. Bend it down and have friends hold it in that position. Now straddle the sapling as close to the top as possible, taking a good grip on the slim trunk. Ready? Then holler, "Let 'er rip!" to the holders; they will all let go at once.

Those could be the directions to a game played by the youngsters of Doucette, which became a thriving sawmill town in the upper portion of the Big Thicket soon after the turn of the century. They named the game Ride the Wild Tree. Sometimes, a youngster got bucked by a sapling with a strong backlash; it would rap back and forth vigorously while the rider tried to hang on. Ride the Wild Tree was a good way to initiate kids to life in a sawmill town.

The Big Thicket forest furnished the playground for boys and girls growing up amid the shrill whine and ever-present yellow dust of the mill. The school yard might have a place for swings, but open fields and woods circling the town provided the main places and the means for having fun. And in the process of having fun, boys and girls learned many of nature's secrets.

Free time was hard to come by. Youngsters were expected to help plough, plant, and harvest food in the home garden or the farm, and to attend school once the work was done. They had even less money than time — in fact, almost no one, including adults, in a sawmill town had money, since mill employees were paid in cards, or scrip, to use for purchases at the company store. The store was owned by the owner of the sawmill. But when a youngster had free time, if the weather was not too cold or too hot, he would likely take off for the woods with friends.

Camping on the creek — Big Turkey Creek, which lay south of Doucette, between that town and Woodville — was a favorite summer pastime for Doucette boys. Each youth carried something to sleep on, usually an old piece quilt since blankets were in short supply, and something to eat with. After a swim, they would make a small fire on the sandy bank and try to catch fish.

Pole fishing was the first method tried. Most boys had stuffed string, hook, and sinker in their pockets. A branch was cut for a pole. Worms were dug for bait. If that combination failed to produce fish, the boys would search for a depression or hole in the creek bed, where they would try to "muddy-up" a few catfish for a meal. Two or three boys would stand waist-deep or chest-deep in the creek with their feet in the depression. Young catfish, "bullhead cats," like to feed in such places. The boys would wiggle their feet and toes in the bottom mud, digging through the muck until the water got cloudy. Soon, if they had chosen the right spot, several catfish would float to the surface, "coming up for air," the boys would say. The lethargic fish were trapped by hand, thrown on the bank, cleaned, and placed in a boiling pot.

Berries, fruits, roots, and nuts gathered in season helped round out a meal in the woods. Hickory nuts, chinquapins, and beech-nuts were favorites, as were blueberries and wild plums. Every boy in Doucette had a syrup bucket for camp cooking and eating, and a two-bladed IXL-brand knife with a tin handle. The IXL cost a dime.

After eating, campers hunted for chewing gum. That meant stretchberry, a small, shiny, black or purplish berry that yields a sweet, chewy substance found wrapped around the seed. Several stretchberries made a good chew. If stretchberries weren't found, sap would be pulled from a sweet gum tree. Flavor was added

35

with crushed sumac berries — not poison sumac, of course, but flame-leaf sumac. Learning to recognize poisonous plants was one of the lessons of woodcraft passed on by older brothers or friends.

Sometimes the lesson didn't sink in. A smart aleck who wanted to act grown-up would make a pipe from a large acorn, hollowed out, and a stem from an elderberry bush. Elderberry stems have a soft, pulpy center that is easy to push out with a thin stick. The smart aleck would then cut a piece of cross-vine, shred it, stuff it into the acorn pipe bowl, light it, and puff happily. If he wasn't careful, or if he didn't know the woods well, he might cut a piece of poison ivy, which grows alongside cross-vine in many places and resembles the "smoking vine." He would suffer from a blistered mouth for several days.

For a snack, campers caught crawfish, or, as they were better known, crawdads. These crustaceans are similar to shrimp in appearance and taste, but have far less flesh. Campers seined them from creeks and ditches filled with water, or caught them on baited strings dropped into crawdad holes, easily recognized by daubed-mud chimneys rising from wet ground. Boiled in clear creekwater and sprinkled with salt, a canful of crawdads made an afternoon munch.

Forest games and activities ranged from tracking animals such as raccoons and possums, climbing eighty-foot-tall trees, and building clubhouses with branches, to competitive games and "wars." The latter included mulberry striping and blowgun battles.

A shrub called the French mulberry produces clusters of soft purple berries about every three inches on a long stem. In a game of Mulberry Massacre, each player cuts a berried switch about three feet long and removes the leaves. That's his weapon. Pants are doffed to expose bare legs. At the signal to begin, the players on each side try to swat the legs of opponents with their mulberry switches, while dodging the others' swipes. A great deal of leaping, falling, and chasing ensues. When a player's legs get striped, dripping the berry "blood," he's out of action.

36

Blowgun battles required chinaberries for ammunition. Guns were made by cutting a one-inch-thick, straight elderberry stalk to a length of eight or ten inches. The pulpy center was reamed out with a stick. A plunger was made by trimming a piece of hardwood branch that had been divided into a rod section and a handle section. The rod part was cut to fit the inside of the elderberry barrel, about one inch shorter than the barrel to allow for two chinaberries. The handle of the rod was sized to fit the user's hand, and a small piece of cloth was wrapped around the tip of the rod to maximize compression. To load the gun, a chinaberry was placed into the rear of the barrel and pushed by the plunger to the other end. A second chinaberry was then loaded into the rear of the elderberry barrel. The gun would now be ready to fire. The tip of the plunger was fitted against the second berry. The plunger was rammed forward. Compression created by the second berry being thrust through the barrel caused the first berry to explode from the other end. To reload, another chinaberry was inserted into the breech.

"The longer the barrel, the better the aim" was a principle of blowgun battles. But ten inches was about the longest practical length. The rules of the game included no shooting at the eyes, and once hit, or hit first in a two-gun standoff, a player was out of action. A well-made blowgun would make a loud slap when fired and raise a welt on the skin of an "enemy" at fifteen feet.

Gars and Minnows made a robust afternoon game at the creek. One boy was chosen as the gar, which is the name of a large fish of the Big Thicket rivers. He took his position in the creek, midway between two agreed-upon tree boundaries. All the other campers lined up on one shore. They were the minnows. At a signal, the minnows tried to swim or thrash to the other side of the creek without getting caught and ducked underwater by the gar. Whoever got victimized by the gar became the next gar. Sometimes a gar would hold a minnow's head underwater too long, resulting in a scrap between the two boys.

If a boy was not permitted by his parents to camp out overnight in the Big Thicket, he would usually try to leave following the afternoon skirmishes at the creek. His mates might not want him to go, or would simply want to pester him in the high spirits of the day. As he would try to get dressed, he might get splattered with a mudball, necessitating the removal of clothes and the taking of another dip to wash off the mud. Two or three repetitions of that prank might start another scrap.

Around the night campfire, talk turned to events at school or in town. As the flames burned low and began sputtering, voices drifted into silence. Boys pulled their quilts tighter about them. If a first-time camper, called a "rookie," was in the group, he would be initiated; that is, suspended somewhere between fascination and fright by tales of wild animals and crazed "lost men" in the Big Thicket deeps. His initiation usually came around midnight, when he had sunk into sleep. Two older or more experienced campers would go a short distance into the brush, where they had spotted a hollow log. Over one end of the log, a piece of thin leather or thick paper would be tied, and a nail stuck through it. A string rubbed with resin was tied to the nail. When the string was stroked, a roaring sound came through the other end of the log. The boys at the campfire would leap awake.

"Panther!" one boy would yell.

"The old bull!" another would holler.

"Aw, it's just the crazy wild man," counseled a third boy. The roaring would grow louder.

"That's a black panther roar if I ever heard one," the first boy persisted.

By this time, the rookie camper would be throwing more wood on the fire to lighten the ominous shadows. At some point, he would discover the absence of the boy or boys who were stationed at the hollow log, and the initiation would be over.

The school year started in the fall after all the cotton had been picked. It ended in the spring, usually early in May, when readying the fields for the new crops required all hands. Many boys took two years to finish each grade because they had to work on the family farm and couldn't be spared for schooling. After age twenty-one, if a boy hadn't graduated, he had to quit. The best baseball players were the twenty-one-year-old boys who were completing their last year in school.

Throughout all grades, subjects included geography, reading, writing, spelling, arithmetic, and conduct. History was added in the higher grades. The superintendent taught the older boys. Women teachers taught the young boys and the girls. Whipping was allowed — six to fifteen licks with a switch cut from a beech tree — when a student was disrespectful. Instead of a whipping by the teacher, a student could choose to be expelled, but if he made that choice, he would have to be prepared for a worse whipping at home.

Most students walked to school. A family was lucky to have a burro that the children could ride. One youngster would ride while the others walked. After a certain distance, they would rotate. Boys wore knee britches or overalls to school; girls wore dresses, usually two sizes too big so that they could grow into them, then hand them down to younger sisters. Students went to school barefooted until the sixth or seventh grade, then wore canvas, or tenny, shoes.

Making spending money was always a problem for both boys and girls. A boy could make fifty cents a day by doing farm work (on somebody else's farm; he didn't get paid for working on his own family farm). Picking cotton in the fall earned fifty cents for every one hundred pounds. The same amount — fifty cents for a day's work must have been the unofficial minimum wage of the times — could be pocketed for cleaning up a lumberyard or a vacant lot. One boy sold the weekly paper *GRIT* and another sold the daily *Chicago Blade & Ledger*. Each sale netted two cents' profit. Other youngsters sold peanuts on "halvers": a boy or girl or a team would pick a volume of peanuts, give half to the farmer, then parch their part and sell it for five cents per pocketful. If a family had a goat, the youngsters could hitch a small wagon to the animal and make spending money by delivering packages for the merchants; or by filling the wagon with rich soil from the woods and selling it by the bucketful to ladies for their flower beds.

Spending money, of course, came in handy for movies — Bronco Billy, Yakima Canutt, and William S. Hart were major heroes — for the traveling Wild West Show that came to town each year, or for the annual carnival. The latter featured whirling cars and a Ferris wheel. The wrestler who traveled with the carnival always provided the most excitement. He would challenge any local man or boy to stay in the ring with him for more than three minutes. If a local male could do that, he would make a dollar a minute thereafter.

Once, at carnival time, a young man of Doucette came home from the navy, where he had learned to wrestle. He accepted the challenge of the carny champ and soon got the big man in a scissors hold. The three-minute time limit passed, and it was costing the champ money. He thrashed around while the Doucette youth tightened the leg grip. He started cursing. The hometown hero didn't appreciate that — his upbringing had taught that some words were inspired by Satan — so he spit on his hands and rubbed them on the "champ's" face.

Without spending money, Doucette kids might cool off in Mr. Cruse's creek. Mr. Cruse would also allow them to pick pears from his orchard and watermelons from his field. He was a stickler for conservation; he showed them the portion of the harvest that he considered correct to provide seed for the following year's crop. After a swim, the gang would often see Mrs. Cruse coming down the path from the house with her apron caught up. It would be full of hot biscuits. Mr. Cruse would bring a half gallon of the cane syrup he put up each year, and a stack of syrup-can lids. Each youngster got a hot biscuit and a lid. Syrup was poured over the biscuit; the lid caught the drippings. When the lid ran full of syrup, it was time for another hot biscuit!

A less cheerful aspect of life in Doucette was illness. "Sore eyes" was a common malady in which the eyes reddened and attracted gnats. The treatment for it was a yellow liquid called

40

Dickie's Eye Water. The most common complaint in town was stepping on a rusty nail. "Look out for lockjaw!" came the warning to the barefooted victim. The puncture, usually in the heel, was soaked in coal oil, then a piece of fat meat was tied over it to draw out any poison.

The worst disease to hit Doucette and other sawmill towns was spinal meningitis. When it struck a young person, the spinal fluid would be drawn off by a needle, then replaced with fluid from the spine of a cow. That operation was performed six times on the patient. Some youths survived the disease and the treatment; some lost an eye to the disease. One boy, Wood Fain, had an infected eye removed so that the disease would not spread to the other healthy eye. The surgery was performed in the doctor's office in Beaumont. Wood's father then took him to a hotel room for a day's recuperation. Two days after the surgery, Wood was riding the sixty miles to his home in a bumpy wagon.

Sawmill towns doomed themselves to extinction. They devastated their own source of supply. As the forests were sawed down and milled into lumber, the towns shriveled and emptied. The big machinery would be disassembled and hauled by train or wagon to a new location, where the process would repeat itself. Sawmill employees would follow behind.

When a half century of uncontrolled lumbering ended in the 1930s, the virgin wilderness of the Big Thicket had been destroyed. On the heels of that era came another industry that battered the remaining wilderness: oil. Oil promised more wealth, overnight, than most men had dreamed possible. And for the "black gold" locked in its subterranean reservoirs, the Big Thicket would be ravaged anew.

CHAPTER 8

𝒦

Derricks and Daredevils

OIL MEANT EXCITEMENT, adventure, and violence. It meant exhilaration and disappointment. It meant the possibility of getting very rich very quick, or going broke very quickly.

Half the crooks, swindlers, gamblers, and gun-for-hire adventurers in the United States swooped down on the Big Thicket oil fields in the early years of this century.

There were actually four oil booms in the Big Thicket. The first started with Spindletop at Beaumont, a city located at the southern edge of the Big Thicket, where the "Age of Petroleum" for the whole world was born. Spindletop was the first well to prove that oil could be produced in immense quantities, enough to power all kinds of engines for untold decades; some observers said the supply was inexhaustible. Within a few years after Spindletop, factories throughout the United States converted their equipment to use oil instead of steam or coal, and oil-burning engines for autos, ships, and trains soon became commonplace. After Spindletop, in quick succession, came the Sour Lake boom, then the Saratoga boom, then the Batson boom.

Long before Spindletop, oil was known to the Indians of the Big Thicket. In a few places it seeped to the surface of the land. They used the dark fluid as medicine, rubbing it on sores, burns, and wounds. Some Indians even sipped oil as a treatment for diseases.

Even before the days of automobiles and other oil-burning

engines, avaricious men were moved to explore for petroleum and willing to fight, slave, lie, and die to possess it. The main reason for its early value was that it provided cheap energy for light.

People wanted to learn, and they needed light at night. They wanted to read the newspapers and magazines and books that were appearing in increasing numbers all over America. They knew that facts, knowledge, and communication of ideas were the true ways toward progress and a better life.

Most Americans in those days worked from sunup to sundown on farms. In the cities, they worked long daylight hours in plants. Home at night, they used candles or firelight for enough visibility to eat supper and prepare for bed. Fire, for those who had a fireplace, meant warmth but little light. Only the rich and well-to-do could afford whale oil for reading lamps.

Partially refined, crude oil, the dark green fluid from the ground, could provide cheap light. With oil, people could read at night after earning the family's keep during the day. The tremendous craving for information, for facts and stories about the world and its widening horizons, was a prime reason for the high value placed on crude oil in the latter part of the nineteenth century.

There were other reasons, of course. America was becoming fascinated with machines. Just a few years before Spindletop, two German men had invented the internal-combustion engine. That invention, coupled with the discovery of huge supplies of oil at Spindletop and other fields that followed, would quickly revolutionize human life all over the world.

The signal for that revolution came at 10:30 on the morning of January 10, 1901, when the Lucas Gusher blew in with a roar at Spindletop, very near the southeastern tip of the Big Thicket.

Spindletop was a small knoll, or rise, in the flat coastal prairie on the south side of Beaumont. A man named Pattillo Higgins believed that oil lay beneath the knoll. Local people thought he was an impractical dreamer. Anthony Lucas, a mining engineer who had migrated to the United States from Austria, agreed with Higgins. Lucas masterminded the plan for drilling the well. The drillers who contracted with Lucas to do the actual work at the rig were two brothers, Al and Curt Hamill, and Peck Byrd. They had drilled wells around Corsicana, in north Texas, and prided themselves on a good reputation. But nobody had ever drilled a well like Spindletop.

From a hole they drilled 1,160 feet into the ground, tons of mud, rocks, gas, and oil exploded several hundred feet into the air. The noise was described as the "sound of a cannon." Then, for several minutes, there was silence. Once more the ground shook, and another explosion shattered the quiet. This time, a greenish liquid spewed skyward. It was oil — more oil than anyone in the world had ever seen flowing before! The countryside was bathed in oil. According to the best calculations, the flow was estimated at 75,000 barrels a day. Much of it was wasted because no one, not even the brilliant Anthony Lucas, knew how to stop the wild flow. For six days, the well poured the dark liquid, creating a huge lake of oil around the derrick. Not until January 19 was the well controlled. On March 3, sparks from a passing locomotive set the lake of oil ablaze. It ignited a series of explosions that rocked the countryside before the fire was choked out.

Did Pattillo Higgins or Anthony Lucas *know* oil existed below Spindletop? Higgins had unlimited faith that it did. Lucas, the engineer, also believed oil was down there. They drilled several dry holes in the vicinity, losing a lot of money on each failure, before the successful well was drilled. The earlier efforts were failures because they didn't go deep enough.

Even today, with the fabulous scientific instruments and techniques that geologists use in exploring for oil and gas under land and under the oceans, there are nine failures, or dry holes, for every successful well.

An oil well was drilled in those days in this manner: First, an entrepreneur or risk taker borrowed or won a lot of money, or got together some rich investors and leased some land he had faith in. He hired a crew of rig builders. They built a derrick and a rig floor, which was a platform beneath the derrick. The derrick

44

itself was a minor masterpiece of carpentry. It was a wooden tower erected over the spot where the well was to be drilled. Rising forty or more feet high, it had to be strong enough to support the heavy drilling machinery. It also had to be tall enough for raising and lowering thirty-foot lengths of pipe, screwed together, and the casing that surrounded the pipe. Pipe and casing were inserted into the hole being drilled. The derrick was cone-shaped with four stout masts connected by lateral braces and crisscross braces about every eight feet of height.

Workers called roughnecks were hired to install the drilling equipment and operate it. Basically, to drill a hole in the ground the equipment needed was a steam-powered engine, a rotary table to turn the drill pipe as it pierced deep into the ground, and the draw works, the equipment that suspended the drill pipe up through the derrick.

As a drill bit chewed deeper and deeper below the surface, lengths of pipe were added. To reduce the pressure and temperature in the well, water was pumped into the hole. It also lubricated the bit, the metal fitting that did the actual boring. When the bit became dull — which was about every day or two — all the pipe would have to be removed, a new bit attached to the drilling assembly, and all the pipe then reinserted into the hole. It was hard, dirty work. And it was dangerous.

Roughnecking meant living a life that "dared the devil to do his damnedest." There was no advance warning when oil was struck. It simply started blowing back out of the well, often mixed with mud and rocks. Sometimes, the pressure could be controlled by valves. At other times, the pressure was too great for that kind of control, and the well, with a tremendous force, spewed a torrent of oil. Such a blowout could kill or maim the crews and destroy the derrick.

After the discovery at Spindletop, bedlam exploded in the Big Thicket. The whole nation knew that it had found the energy substitute for coal and steam. Land around Spindletop was hawked — and sold — for as much as $900,000 an acre.

Months later, when Spindletop had quieted down somewhat,

45

the "boomers" flocked to a town called Sour Lake, fourteen miles northwest of Beaumont, into the real midst of the Big Thicket. Sour Lake had been known for its mineral springs. During the 1850s it had become a famous health resort; the aging war hero Sam Houston came to Sour Lake to take the mineral baths and ease the pain of his war wounds. Now it became famous for its oil.

Seventeen miles north of Sour Lake, in the village of Saratoga, a third oil field was discovered in the same year, 1901. Saratoga was named after the world-famous spa in New York state because it, too, offered hot mineral waters for the relief of the aches and pains of its visitors. Many years later, the village would become well known as the home of Lance Rosier, who inspired the fight to save the Big Thicket.

The prize for the roughest and rowdiest town of all in those boom days would have to have gone to Batson, seven miles west of Saratoga. The town's saloons stayed open for business twenty-four hours a day; in fact, saloons didn't even bother to have doors. Fistfights and gunfights kept the jail wagon to Kountze, twenty-three miles away, on a constant run, and overloaded with offenders on each trip. Most of Batson's fortune hunters lived in ragtowns — acres of tents and shacks made of rags. Shootings occurred about as often as someone became a millionaire and someone else went broke from drilling a dry hole, which was daily.

One day, as the story of the discovery of the Batson field goes, a boy named Ed Cotten and his wagon were hired by a Beaumont man named Steve Pipkin to take him out to the Batson prairie. They drove to a spot where Pipkin cut a stick from a persimmon tree and started making a hole in the ground with it. Then he got a tin can, cut out the bottom of it, and placed the crude funnel over the hole. He lit a match and held it over the funnel. Poof! There was a tiny explosion. He repeated the experiment a number of times, then had the Cotten boy drive him back to town.

Pipkin, according to the story, was checking out a report given to him and to another man by Judge W. L. Douglas. Douglas had

46

gone hunting around Batson, barefooted, and had gotten his feet dirty. The dirt was loaded with paraffin. He knew he had come across something that indicated oil. Hustling back to Beaumont, the judge visited two wealthy lumbermen who had money to invest, and showed them the waxy dirt on his still-bare feet. One of the lumbermen was Steve Pipkin, who went to investigate the judge's tale. The persimmon stick and the tin-can funnel made a satisfactory test. A well was drilled, and on October 31, 1901, the drilling bit struck oil. After that, the Batson boom was on.

Indian Joe, Big Thicket Kid, Notchcutter, Broomface, Hambone, and Six Shooter Kate were the names of some of the leading characters of Batson's boom days.

Since the police wagon to the Kountze jail couldn't hold all the accused offenders on its daily runs, the overflow defendants were chained to trees until the wagon could return to Batson and pick them up. That might take a day or two, depending on the condition of the roads. In wet weather, it was not unusual for whole teams of mules and oxen to get stuck so deep in mud that they were immobilized for several days. The mud was so thick that the owners of the two hotels in Batson had to use hoes instead of brooms to clean the floors.

"Per capita," says Big Thicket cowboy and folklorist Bill Brett, "Batson probably had more killin's and less done about it than any of the boomtowns."

Violence was usually a matter of gunplay and raw whiskey that set off bad tempers, but on occasion it took different forms. One day, a man named Raibee was caught butchering a stolen cow. The ranchers who caught him completed the butchering process, then sewed him up in the wet hide and left him out on the prairie — so the story goes.

Conditions grew so dangerous in Batson that the Texas Rangers were asked to enforce law and order in the once-sleepy little village. Without even sewage facilities, not to mention enforceable laws, it had become home to thousands of roughnecks, roustabouts, gamblers, gunmen, and assorted would-be millionaires.

The Rangers sent one man to Batson, Captain J. A. Brooks, in accordance with the principle "one riot, one Ranger." By 1906, the situation was under control. Law-abiding citizens had formed a Good Government League. Local officials, some of whom were taking under-the-table money, and bad characters both got firm treatment from Ranger Captain Brooks.

The oil field was soon drained. Then, when a discovery was made in Humble, Texas, eighty miles away, near Houston, the boomers pulled up stakes at Batson and hightailed it to the town of Humble to seek their elusive fortunes once again.

The oil booms left ugly marks on parts of the Big Thicket wilderness that had managed to escape the lumberjack's ax. Salt water, overflowing from the oil wells, killed large areas of vegetation, expanses that today remain bare wasteland. Black scum stained the flowering meadows. In one place, near Sour Lake, the pumping of oil from its underground reservoir caused the earth's surface actually to sink, creating a crater one hundred forty feet deep and fifteen acres wide. Gas escaped from drilling holes and moved through the forests, poisoning plants and wildlife, spoiling nesting areas for both land birds and exotic water birds. Deep gouges were cut into the massive loblolly pine and mixed forests for derrick lumber and shantytown buildings. And while the quest for black gold wrought its particular kind of havoc in the southern realms of the Thicket, the timber industry continued its massive cutting at an ever-faster pace throughout the entire region.

Doom for Big Thicket wilderness, once a primeval marvel of nature, appeared imminent. But before it became famous as a battleground for conservationists who wanted to save its remaining wilderness and commercial interests that wanted to exploit its forests and minerals, the Big Thicket would catch America's imagination as a jungle where black bears, sometimes weighing five hundred to six hundred pounds, roamed and roared. Men came from across the United States to hunt them.

Sandbar in Village Creek. Pure whiteness of these sandbars gave
an Indian name for "snow" to the nearby river, Neches.

Large boulders in upper Thicket, reminiscent of New England woods

Snakemouth orchid, found
in seeps; becoming rare
through loss of habitat

Sassafras sapling. One
of two tree species that
produce four different leaf
shapes. Leaves were used by
woodsmen to quench their
thirst on long treks.

Wild silky camellia. Very rare; only one grove remains in the Big Thicket.

Flower of the loblolly pine

Rattan vine encircling large tree

Streambottom hardwood forest scene

Community of pitcher plants
and royal ferns. Meat-eating
pitcher plant is very recent on
the evolutionary scale;
royal fern very primitive.

"Toothache tree." Inner bark
used by pioneers to deaden pain
of toothache or sore gums.

Sprouts of the Pyramid magnolia.
Rare and endangered species
in the Big Thicket.

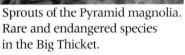

Wild magnolias form a dominant
ecosystem with beech trees
and loblolly pines

Magnolia bloom. Ancient species; one of the first plants
to devise seed with hard covering, not "naked" seed.

Acidbog-baygall scene

Alligator Pond. A succession pond in arid sandylands
that will evolve into acidbog-baygall.

Ancient cypress "sculpture"
in the Neches River Bottom

In snowy woods, an oxbow
cutoff from a nearby creek

Palmetto-hardwood forest scene

Leafy floor of beech-magnolia-loblolly forest

Waterfall and pool with sandbar in longleaf pine uplands

Collecting palmettos in oil-boom days, early 1900s. Big Thicket palmetto
leaves were shipped north in large numbers for Christmas decorations.
Palmettos once grew high enough for a person to ride beneath on horseback.

Drilling for oil at Batson, early 1900s

Main Street, Batson. Rowdy oil-boom days, early 1900s.

A Batson prisoner, oil-boom days. Lawbreakers were
often chained to trees to await the jail wagon.

Logging crew in early days of Big Thicket timbering

Virgin pine forest c. 1900

Bill Brett. Present-day
Big Thicket cowboy,
folklorist, and novelist.

Ben Lilly — America's
greatest bear hunter — on a
hunt in the Big Thicket

Former U.S. Congressman Bob Eckhardt and "Mr. Big Thicket," Lance Rosier. Rosier was often honored for his role in the "Save the Big Thicket" effort.

KEITH OZMORE

Young people enjoy outings in the woods today as much as ever. This group from Woodville pauses beneath a large beech tree for a snapshot. Standing left to right are Teresa Cook, Jill Spurlock, and Kelly Craine; sitting are Rodney Cook, Martin Houston, and Ashley Poindexter.

CHAPTER 9

𝒦

Bear Hunt

A BEAR HUNT in the Big Thicket headed by the famous hunter Ben Lilly became a classic story of its time. Written in December 1906 by a Kansas journalist named A. L. Kiene, it first appeared in the *Topeka State Journal* but soon gained wide circulation in the eastern and midwestern parts of the nation.

A traditional Big Thicket hunt such as Kiene describes usually began at dawn after bacon and biscuits and pots of coffee had been consumed around a campfire. The success of the hunt depended on the skill and woodlore of the hosts, the Hooks brothers Bud and Ben, both experienced hunters and natives of the region, and on their hounds, which were conceded by other hunters to be the best bear-hunt team in the surrounding country. The lead hounds were Old Bugle and Dandy.

On this particular outing, however, a potent new element was added: the presence of Ben Lilly, the most renowned bear hunter in all America. (A year after the Big Thicket hunt, the President of the United States, Theodore Roosevelt, would name Lilly as his Chief Huntsman for a bear hunt in Louisiana.) He had joined the hunting party in Kountze, a small community located near a place in the forest called "The Hurricane." There, trees a hundred feet tall and higher, hundreds of years old, had been uprooted and thrown down by a storm. The tangled trunks formed a framework for vines and brush that quickly covered the area, creating an ideal habitat for many kinds of animals. The Hurricane was in the heart of bear country.

Lilly, a native of Louisiana, had been hired by the U.S. Biological Survey to collect specimens for the National Museum. Having already accounted for one hundred seventeen bears, probably a national record then that today would be an international outrage, he joined the Big Thicket party to try to obtain a large museum specimen. His reputation was imposing. So was the man himself.

Possessing the physique of an Olympic athlete, he was hard-muscled, broad-shouldered, barrel-chested, slim in the waist and hips, with unbelievably powerful arms and legs. He admitted to fifty years of age.

Lilly's physical achievements made most folk heroes pale in comparison. He could run great distances without being winded. Chasing a bear one day through a swampy area, he lost a shoe in the mud, ran the bear at top speed through the woods for almost twelve miles before cornering the creature — then went back and got his shoe. He couldn't swim, but was so long-winded and powerful that he walked underwater, using a gun or pole for ballast. He never took off wet clothes, contending it was healthful to let them dry on the body. He was known to sleep in the crotch of a tree, like a turkey, during a storm, because the water-covered ground was not fit to sleep on. He would walk miles to obtain clean drinking water, believing it to be the secret of health. If a friend caught a cold, Lilly built a fire of horse manure and advised his friend to breathe the smoke; he claimed the fumes would cure any respiratory disease. He used the treatment himself once when ailing with pneumonia.

In contrast to his overpowering physical strength, Ben Lilly spoke in a gentle voice, used old-fashioned manners and courtesies in dealing with others, never cursed or told an off-color story, and would not listen to others who did so. He refused to do any work on Sunday and would not participate in any activity on that day of the week. His face, according to Big Thicket people who knew him, always wore a cheerful expression, as if he was keeping some funny story or high jinks bottled up inside.

"Ben never got lost in the woods," Big Thicket old-timers still say. "You could turn him around a dozen times in a jungle he'd never seen before, and he still knew exactly where he was. On top of that, he was one of the funniest guys you ever went camping with . . . ."

They say Ben Lilly would ride a horse at a full gallop through a grove of trees, catch a low-hanging branch, clamber up the trunk and branches as fast as a squirrel, and all the time be squawking in perfect imitation of his bush-tailed friends. They also report that he could stand in a barrel and jump out of it flatfooted.

Lilly spent his later years in the west, hunting in Texas, Mexico, Arizona, and New Mexico. He became known as the master sign reader of the Rocky Mountains, the last and one of the greatest and most fearless of the legendary mountain men.

Now, for A. J. Kiene's story — shortened considerably — of a Big Thicket bear hunt.

Ben Hooks is the master of the hunt. He manages the dogs and can come nearer to keeping up with them than anyone. He is a little less than forty years old, as lithe as a greyhound, with the endurance of a well-trained athlete. He is well educated and rich, for he knew just when to dispose of his oil properties in the Beaumont fields. Bud, his younger brother, is heavier on his feet; he has a monstrous head covered with iron gray hair, and a ready wit. He is the life of the camp, for he is never too weary to tell a good story or enjoy a practical joke. Like his brother, he got out of "oil" in time and has the money and leisure to enjoy himself and entertain his friends. He has a charming family and his cozy home is surrounded by pens in which there are tame deer, wild geese, and a pair of year-old black bear. They are princes in their own realm. . . .

Dandy [the start dog] is nine years old, entirely deaf, slow of motion, but still the head, the most important dog in the [eight-dog] pack. He is a monster hound, probably containing a strain

51

of cur. He is utterly oblivious to every track but that of the bear. He has an unfailing scent and once he strikes a trail he never quits. . . .

A trail in the Big Thicket is a path cut through the forests and tangle of underbrush and usually marked by blazed trees. It is easy enough to follow in the dense jungles, because there is no place else that will permit the free passage of a human being, but in the open forests and "burnouts" it is often difficult to find; and once off the trail a tenderfoot is helpless.

Ben Hooks and Mr. Lilly were in charge of "the drive." The other members of the party were posted where the bear might cross the trails. The drivers, with the aid of Dandy, were supposed to find the bear and start the chase. John Salters and the writer were mounted and the rest were on foot. A horse can be ridden on the trails if the rider does not object to having his knees and shins bumped by trees, but in the Thicket a horse is next to useless to one little used to riding. . . .

It was about 7:40 o'clock when the hunt began at the Hurricane, and it was nearly an hour later before Dandy lifted up his voice in the welcome though discordant notes that signaled that his quest [finding the track of a bear] had been successful. The trail was a hot one and in a few minutes the deep and infrequent baying of the old dog became almost a yelp, which told that the quarry had "jumped," or had left his lair. This was the signal for releasing the pack. . . .

Mr. Lilly then gave the writer the following instructions: "Ride down to the Buck Pond and then south toward Black Creek, he may come back that way, and if he does you will meet him. . . ." The Buck Pond was about two miles away by the trail and in that direction the tenderfoot from Kansas made his way.

When the writer reached the Buck Pond, riding slowly, he stopped, and far ahead he heard the yelping of the pack. At the risk of smashing a knee cap or two, he spurred the horse to a gallop. . . .

(Here, near Buck Pond, as Lilly had predicted, the bear was brought to bay by Kiene and the pack of hounds.)

Every man who hunts in the Big Thicket is equipped with a horn which is made of an ordinary steer's horn, scraped thin and with the tip end sawed off. This can be heard three or four miles after one becomes accustomed to blowing it, and it is the signal of the huntsman. Here is the code: three long blasts means "come to me"; and two blasts means "answer me"; one blast is used to call the dogs. The Kansan is not an expert at blowing a hunting horn, but he blew three blasts until it seemed as if his lips would drop off and no one answered. He fired his rifle and shouted until he was hoarse, but there was no response. An hour passed and then far down toward Black Creek, the deep baying of Dandy was heard. The veteran hound soon came up and he forgot his age long enough to caper around. . . .

Ten minutes after the arrival of Dandy, the hunter got an answer to his horn. . . .

Dogs are seldom used for two days in succession during a bear hunt. Unlike a deer, bruin keeps to the dense thickets when followed by dogs, and the underbrush and briars lacerate the skins of the hounds until the dogs become too careful to be effective. They also become foot-sore from long races. They are also often injured by the bear. During one fight last season six dogs out of eight in the chase were disabled by a big bear that weighed six hundred pounds. They all recovered, however.

The hunt ended after the party had been in the woods for almost nine hours without food or drink. Kiene concludes:

The passing of the North American black bear is only a question of a few years. . . . Mr. Lilly, who has spent the greater portion of his life hunting, says that there are only fifteen bear left in the Big Thicket and that there are but forty in all the southern bear territory, including Texas, Louisiana, Mississippi, and Arkansas.

The Big Thicket was originally about a hundred miles long and thirty miles wide, but the axe of the lumberman has reduced it . . . and even now the giant pines are being felled within three-quarters of a mile of the Parker house, the hunting headquarters of the Hooks. When the forests are no more the doom of the few surviving members of the big game family in the South will have been sounded; and this time is not far away.

The black bear was a magnificent animal, and the forests and people of the Thicket are poorer by its elimination through hunting and loss of habitat. Unfortunately, it was not the only magnificent creature to be destroyed by human ignorance and deadly sport.

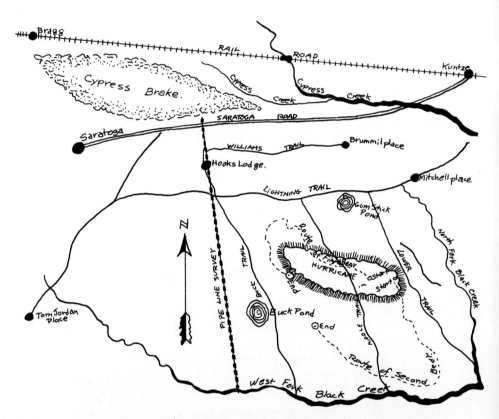

Site of the bear hunt. Drawn by Kelly Asbury, from Saul Aronow's map. Original map of the site, currently in the possession of Esther Hooks Walker, was drawn by Bud Hooks.

CHAPTER 10

𝄢

Gone Forever?

"A LOUD RUSHING ROAR, succeeded by instant darkness."* That was the way a Scottish ornithologist, Alexander Wilson, visiting America in 1810, described a flight of passenger pigeons.

There were so many birds in the flock, stretching almost from horizon to horizon, that he decided to count them. It took one whole day for the flock to pass over him.

The Scotsman was skilled at numbers. He timed the speed of the birds, then estimated the number of individual birds in a cubic yard of air. From that point it was a matter of clocking the flight. When the last passenger pigeon passed overhead, he did the calculation. The total was 2,230,272,000 birds. One flock: well over two *billion* birds.

John James Audubon, a renowned naturalist and probably the world's most admired painter of birds, watched a flight of passenger pigeons in Kentucky during his travels in 1813. By his expert figuring, that flock totaled one billion plus. For three days flocks of pigeons continued. "The light of noon-day was obscured as by an eclipse," he wrote.

Today, not a single passenger pigeon lives on earth. Only a stuffed skin remains on display in the Smithsonian Institution, in Washington, D.C., to show us what a passenger pigeon looked

* © 1963. American Heritage Publishing Company, Inc. Reprinted by permission from Natural Wonders.

like. This last bird, named Martha, died in 1914 in the Cincinnati zoo.

Passenger pigeons lived in the Big Thicket in huge numbers. To the east of the forest where the Ben Lilly bear hunt took place, about five miles south of present-day Kountze, a particular broad clearing there is known as Pigeon Roost Prairie. Old-timers say that beech trees, oaks, hickories, and other food trees once circled this prairie and attracted millions of passenger pigeons.

This beautiful creature — about eighteen inches long, with blue and rust-colored plumage and a snowy breast — was America's most populous bird. Authorities estimate conservatively that at one time at least five billion passenger pigeons flew the nation's skies. Probably there were many more than that number. How did people manage to wipe them out?

Masses of passenger pigeons were killed to supply restaurants with squab. Masses more were killed because they damaged crops. Masses more were killed "just for the sport of it." Still, Americans thought the supply was endless.

The supply ended in 1900, when a hunter in Ohio shot the last known wild passenger pigeon. A few, including Martha, were kept in zoos. But they refused to breed in captivity. They all died.

Today, the story of the passenger pigeon is being repeated in many ways around the world, including the Big Thicket. Some of nature's most magnificent creations are threatened with extinction — the tiger, the snow leopard, the elephant, the whale, the giraffe. Nature needed thirteen million years to evolve the giraffe; yet in a short time, the only way to see these fantastic animals may be in pictures.

Two of the Big Thicket's most impressive creatures, the bear and the panther, have probably disappeared from its forests. They exist elsewhere — but for how long? The same question may soon be asked of the playful river otter, the red wolf (only fifty or so individuals remain in the wild, and another twenty or so in a Tacoma, Washington, zoo), and even the bobcat. At one time, bobcats were so numerous that they were considered local pests. Few people seemed to care that the bobcat kept rodents under control, and that at least half of its diet consisted of animals harmful to homes, farms, and people. But a few years ago European fur dealers discovered the beauty of the bobcat's pelt. They began offering high prices for these dramatically marked skins. In the year 1976–1977 alone, more than 100,000 bobcats were trapped or killed for the international fur-coat market.

Since human beings invented civilization, about two hundred species of animals have disappeared from the globe, according to scientists who keep track. In America, some one hundred kinds of animals are close to extinction. The record for plants is not encouraging, either. In round numbers, about twenty thousand species of plants live in America. Of these, twelve hundred are threatened and about seven hundred fifty are on the brink of extinction, a number of them holding out in the Big Thicket. Already, about a hundred plant species have completely disappeared from the earth.

In response to the growing alarm expressed by nature lovers and scientists over the threats to plant and animal life in America, and in many places throughout the world, the U.S. Congress took action. Laws were passed in 1966, 1969, and 1973 that try to protect endangered species. In many ways, the laws are effective. But who can keep a hunter from firing a shot at a whooping crane, if he or she knows — or doesn't know — the priceless value and rare status of "America's most magnificent bird." Who can keep a garden club member on a field trip in the Big Thicket from marking the location of a rare wild orchid, then stealing back the next day to dig it up and place it in a city garden where it will surely die?

The biggest woodpecker in America was, or is, the ivorybill. No one knows whether the ivory-billed woodpecker is extinct or whether, in the depths of the Big Thicket or some nearby wilderness, a few individuals might still live. It grew, or grows, up to two feet long from bill to tail. It was, or is, so big that when it hammered a tree trunk in the Big Thicket, searching for grubs, old-timers say you could hear the sound for miles if the wind was right.

Every so often, someone will say he or she has seen the ivorybill in the Thicket. Most of the time, these viewers have seen the pileated woodpecker, which looks quite a bit like the ivorybill, but even at a huge fifteen inches long is not as large as the "king 'pecker." Occasionally, a knowledgeable naturalist will report a sighting of the ivorybill. But it is not publicly confirmed by an ornithologist, for fear that someone might find the spot and shoot the last survivors of this species. Some individuals take pleasure in that kind of destruction.

One scientist, Dr. George M. Woodwell of Massachusetts, puts the problem of endangered species into a few words: "Studies show that the diversity of species and human welfare are inextricably related."

If some scientists are right, mankind hurts itself when it wipes out another life form on earth, be it plant or animal. And no matter how numerous a life form may be, numbers alone are not enough to assure survival. Five billion passenger pigeons were not enough. No longer does the creaking-windmill call and tree-trunk pounding of the ivory-billed woodpecker resound through the forests. No longer is the growl of the black bear heard in the baygalls and cypress and palmetto sloughs of the Big Thicket deeps.

By the 1960s, very little time remained to save the beauty and priceless value of the Big Thicket. The crucial forests were being cut at a faster rate than ever. The stage was set for a hero, and an unlikely one appeared.

CHAPTER 11

Save the Big Thicket

A SMALL CIRCUS once came to stage a one-night show for the people of the Big Thicket living in the Kountze-Saratoga area, before moving on to the cities nearby. Overnight an old baboon in the circus died. Instead of burying him, the circus owners, anxious to be on their way, put the body of the animal in a ditch.

The story goes that the men who discovered the body didn't know what it was, but they figured Lance Rosier, a self-taught naturalist who lived in Saratoga, could identify it. He was forever finding out things about animals and plants. They got word to him to come on over and put the right name to the discovery.

Rosier looked at the carcass, rubbed his chin, and intoned in a serious voice: "Considering his stooped posture, the frown on his face, and the calluses on his rump, I'd say he was a Big Thicket domino player."

Lance Rosier's rustic wit came naturally. He was born in a cabin in the woods a few miles southeast of Saratoga. When his family moved away, he went to live with an aunt in an old vine-covered, weathered-pine building, which became a boarding house and was his home for most of his life.

The villagers looked at the boy and figured he'd never amount to much. While other boys played ball, he went to the woods or the meadows. They taunted him because he'd rather study birds than shoot them. The gibes of his schoolmates might or might not have hurt, but while he danced with style and learned to play the piano well, he stayed quite happy alone. He never married, and he was apt to take off for the woods any day, any time. He once left on a jaunt of several days with only a cold sweet potato in his pocket, depending on wild berries and nuts to satisfy any hunger pangs. As a man, he earned a modest living as a timber estimator and as a guide for surveyors who were baffled by the Big Thicket.

The turning point in Rosier's life as a naturalist came in 1936, when two prominent scientists, H. B. Parks and V. L. Cory, set up an expedition for cataloging the extraordinary variety of plant and animal life of the Big Thicket. Week after week, Rosier took them into various realms of the Thicket that he had roamed and studied all his life. In turn, they taught him how to use scientific "keys" for identifying plants of all kinds, and helped him learn the correct but difficult Latin names.

"When you use the scientific name," they pointed out, "every scientist in the world knows what you're talking about, or can look it up. But when you use a popular name, only the people in your area might know it by that name. The people in the next state, or even in the next county, might have another name for a particular flower or bird or tree."

Soon after the publication in 1938 of *Biological Survey of the East Texas Big Thicket Area*, by Cory and Parks, biologists and botanists throughout the United States took note of the Thicket and came calling on Lance Rosier. He had gained a reputation as an extremely knowledgeable, though self-educated, guide. One scientist referred him to another, and the chain kept growing.

Classes of schoolchildren also began asking Rosier to take them on hikes in the woods. Writers, artists, poets, and outdoors people heard of the Big Thicket and Lance Rosier, and arrived in Saratoga without notice. Often he would be found on the porch of the old Vines Hotel. If a visitor expressed genuine interest in the Thicket, Rosier would put on his battered hat, and away into the woods they would go.

"Lance was especially fond of young students and children," a friend says. "He would be apt to give them just as much time, and just as much patience, as he would give a world-famous scientist or politician. Maybe more!"

For over thirty years, until 1969, Rosier guided people into the woods and inspired them with a respect and enthusiasm for nature. To the best of anyone's knowledge, he refused only once to take a visitor on a field trip. That man said if Rosier would only show him where a certain rare bird could be found, he could shoot it and make a nice amount of money by selling the bird's carcass.

Lance Rosier knew the location of an active ivory-billed woodpecker nest, though even then the bird was considered extinct.

He also had a pet crow named Richard. A Houston newspaper columnist was visiting Rosier one day when the crow flew up and perched on Lance's shoulder. In his polite way, Rosier introduced the bird to the reporter.

"Glad to meet you, Richard," the reporter said, playing the game.

"Howdy!" responded Richard. The reporter jumped in surprise. Like mynah birds, crows can be taught to speak.

Rosier was to become a hero in the long fight to save parts of the Thicket, but he didn't look the role. He was short and wiry, about five feet five and 125 pounds. He was rejected by the U.S. Army in his youth because he weighed only 117 pounds, and the army figured he wasn't strong enough. They didn't know how strong he was. Even in his old age, he outlasted young men on long, rugged walks into the Big Thicket woods. His companions would be panting and dragging; he would just be hitting his stride. Everywhere he went he wore a beat-up hat, brim turned up. He spoke in a gentle voice, often with wry humor. To top off this unlikely portrait of a Texas hero, rarely in his eighty-four years did he venture more than a dozen miles from home.

"Going into the woods with Lance was like entering a new and wonderful world," a Big Thicket visitor said. "He knew the birds and animals, the trees and flowers, as friends. Through him, you saw and felt nature in a way you had never imagined it before." Rosier once kept a copperhead snake charmed by slowly moving his arm over the snake's head, so that a scientist could observe the snake's coloring. Then he patted the copperhead on its back and wished it well on its way.

Scientists from many of America's great universities — Harvard, Columbia, Texas A&M, to name a few — came to see the Big Thicket and learn its wonders from Lance Rosier. They also came from foreign lands — Norway, Belgium, Venezuela, Japan. He gave his time freely. Famous writers came calling for stories. And a distinguished justice of the United States Supreme Court, William O. Douglas, went into the woods with Lance Rosier and came out a dedicated champion for the cause of saving the Big Thicket. Douglas wrote a book about the natural endowments of Texas, and his first chapter was devoted to the Thicket and Lance Rosier.

How did this unassuming little man attract so many scientists and knowledgeable people to the sleepy village of Saratoga? Was he a man of vast education? The answer is yes and no.

He never got past high school in Saratoga, but he never stopped learning. For most of his life, he ordered books from the public library. And he kept his reference books well thumbed. Plant by plant, bird by bird, animal by animal, he learned about nature by reading and from firsthand observation in the wilds of the Big Thicket. He once observed, from a hidden position, what woodsmen call an "armadillo funeral." Only a few Big Thicket natives have reported this phenomenon, in which several armadillos circle a dead member of their species. One animal eventually steps out of the circle and with its powerful claws begins digging a trench beside the dead armadillo. The others watch. It doesn't take the digger long; armadillos are instinctive rooters. When the hole is large enough, the dead animal is rolled into it. Dirt is pushed back over the body, then leaves and leaf mold. Then, the animals quickly scatter.

On his own initiative, Rosier memorized scientific names of plants and animals in Latin and Greek as well as their down-home names, how they lived, what peculiarities they had. He never boasted about all he knew; he always figured there was more to learn. Even in his eighties, he considered himself a student.

During his lifetime Rosier watched much of the Thicket disappear. Acre upon acre of woods were wiped out by the growth of towns and villages, farms and ranches. Timber companies, oil producers, and other commercial interests multiplied and took a terrific toll. They required not only that land be cleared of trees and understory — low vegetation — but also that huge quantities of lumber be milled for construction purposes. In addition, industry in the northern and eastern United States consumed as much Big Thicket lumber as the sawmills could produce. By the 1950s, the original 3.5 million acres of primitive wilderness had been reduced to a mere few hundred thousand acres. Decades had passed since anyone had reported sighting a bear. Only a few panthers remained, and the stands of pine and hardwood were virtually gone. An attempt in the 1930s to form an organization of citizens to save parts of the Big Thicket had failed because of the distractions and demands of the Great Depression, followed by World War II and the postwar building boom. But in 1964, inspired and encouraged by Lance Rosier, a handful of citizens formed an organization called the Big Thicket Association to try to save what was left for a national park or preserve. Their cause was dramatized by the shocking story of the Witness Tree.

A giant magnolia tree, perhaps a thousand years old, dominated one of the Thicket's wildest areas. No doubt the Indians had used it for a ceremonial site. The tree was so imposing that three counties were mapped to meet only a few feet from its base. It was called the Witness Tree because it had witnessed the passage of Indian tribes into Texas territory, the explorations of Sieur de La Salle, and the coming of the early settlers.

In 1966, when U.S. Supreme Court Justice William O. Douglas arranged for Rosier to take him on a Big Thicket field trip, Rosier included the Witness Tree site. Only a whited stump, fifty feet high and four feet thick, remained. Someone had bored five holes at the base of the giant tree and poured deadly poison, arsenate of lead, into the ancient giant.

63

"Why?" asked the Supreme Court justice, aghast.

"To protest the idea of a national park for the Big Thicket."

"Who would do that kind of thing?"

Rosier is said to have answered: "The kind of person who killed President Kennedy."

After the story of the Witness Tree received publicity throughout Texas and many parts of the United States, largely as a result of Douglas's field trip and book, titled *Farewell to Texas*, memberships in the Big Thicket Association grew steadily, and contributions for saving the Big Thicket's remaining wilderness increased.

In the early spring of 1970, Rosier was hospitalized. The small, hunched body that had moved tirelessly through the Big Thicket for decades, ahead of children and college students and learned scientists and writers and great political leaders, died on March 12, 1970.

When news of Lance Rosier's death reached Washington, the U.S. Senate paid tribute to this humble naturalist and his lifelong efforts to save the Big Thicket. The lengthy tribute was printed in the *Congressional Record* of March 12, 1970, under the heading DEATH FELLS MR. BIG THICKET.

The Big Thicket Association grew a thousand members strong. Those who had been inspired by Lance Rosier inspired others. National leaders appeared: U.S. Senator Ralph W. Yarborough and U.S. Congressman Bob Eckhardt were among the first and most forceful. Writers and photographers captured the beauty and uniqueness of the Big Thicket and spread the word. Ministers offered prayers and exhortations. The association won a national $10,000 American Heritage contest, and the money was used to buy an old school building for a headquarters and Big Thicket Museum. Magazine stories and pictures called America's attention to the need for saving the Big Thicket: *Life, Science, Audubon, American Forests, National Geographic,* and many others covered the story. Hundreds of people, then thousands, began showing up at the museum in Saratoga to see what all the fuss was about. Field guides took them into the woods and fields to show them.

Two of those field guides were Harold Nicholas, a native of Saratoga and protégé of Lance Rosier, and Geraldine Watson of Silsbee, a native of the Thicket who became one of its most effective and ardent champions. Loyal volunteers kept the museum open and the association operating. Efforts mushroomed. Progressive business and industry leaders gave aid and influence. And on October 11, 1974, legislation authored by Congressman Charles Wilson of Lufkin, which was approved by both the House of Representatives and the Senate, was signed into law by President Gerald Ford. It was the first legislation ever passed in the United States creating a national preserve — the 84,550-acre Big Thicket National Preserve.

The new term *preserve* had been suggested by National Park Service officials to distinguish sanctuaries such as the Big Thicket from established national parks, which include both highly developed facilities as well as extensive wilderness.

Skirmishes with those who opposed saving the Thicket were not completely over. Some unlawful tree cutting would continue for a while. Efforts would be made to delay purchase by the U.S. government of designated acres. While much work remained to complete what the legislative victory had begun, Big Thicket supporters and nature lovers everywhere could pause for a moment to take stock.

CHAPTER 12

Forests for Recreation and Commerce

THE BIG THICKET contains three kinds of forests — recreational forests, commercial forests, and wild forests. In some places they lie near or next to each other; in other places they are miles apart, separated by towns and ranches. The Big Thicket National Preserve is dedicated to the wild forest only.

Most people are familiar with the first kind, the recreational forest, which is maintained and operated purely for outdoor pleasure. A good example in the Thicket is Martin Dies, Jr., State Park, located on the Neches River about fifteen miles east of Woodville. It spreads over seven hundred acres of lush woodlands, dominated by large evergreens and deciduous trees, and offers a wide variety of activities for family camping.

Swimming in the river, which has a sandy-silt bottom; water-skiing and boating; fishing from a lighted pier at midnight, with only night calls from creatures in the nearby woods to break the silence (unless another fisherman on the pier grumbles about losing bait to a cagey bass); screened shelters with electricity and water; clean restrooms with hot and cold showers; boat-launching ramps — these are among the features that make a recreational forest extremely popular for vacations and family holidays.

Bass, perch, and catfish put up a spirited fight for anglers on the banks of the Neches and other Thicket rivers and streams; all make tasty fried panfish for a campfire dinner, dressed out with

66

sliced fresh tomatoes, coleslaw, green onions, and hush puppies.

Hush puppies make a story in themselves. Some people keep their recipes for hush puppies a secret. There is even a Hush Puppy Olympics held each year in the city of Lufkin, north of the Big Thicket area, where hundreds of people pit their recipes and cooking skills against one another's. Passersby enjoy samples from each contestant's fry pot.

A hush-puppy mix can be bought at a supermarket or made from scratch. Here is Boyd McGaugh's recipe, which won the 12th Annual Hush Puppy Olympics in 1983:

> Mix:
> 2 cups white cornmeal
> 2 Tablespoons flour
> 3 eggs
>
> Salt and pepper to taste
>
> Add:
> 1 bunch green onions (about 6 stalks), chopped
> 1 whole white onion, chopped
>
> Mix with whole milk until tacky
>
> Add:
> 1 Tablespoon jalapeño peppers, chopped
>
> Heat Crisco shortening. Fry a few pieces of catfish
> in the shortening, then add the hush-puppy batter,
> using a round butter scoop for an even shape. Cook
> until golden brown.

The marvelous flavor of these morsels must have something to do with the catfish.

In addition to extensive facilities for the pleasure and comfort of campers and vacationers, a good recreational forest will also offer nature trails with interpretation programs.

The Big Thicket's commercial forests and wilderness forests

contrast greatly with the recreational forests, and also differ tremendously from one another.

Commercial forests, which are grown for lumber and other marketable products, begin as desolate fields. These tracts have been clear-cut, a term used to describe the process of uprooting every tree, shrub, and plant, then pushing them into long piles called windrows, and burning the debris.

When this preliminary clearing has been completed, the fields, which might stretch over hundreds of acres, will be sprigged with pine seedlings. Using a mechanical planter, a crew of workers can plant thousands of pine seedlings in a single day. In about seventeen to twenty years, the seedlings will grow to market-size trees. They will then be cut and loaded aboard log trucks for transport to nearby lumber mills. There they are converted to building materials, paper pulp, or any number of more than five thousand products ranging from soap and chewing gum to the nose cones of spaceships. The vehicles that carried U.S. astronauts into outer space were fitted with wooden cones that could withstand reentry temperatures up to 5,000 degrees Fahrenheit. Major lumber companies invest large sums of money in developing seedlings that are resistant to disease and insects, and that grow faster, taller, and straighter than the older species. Trees that show these superior qualities will be used for cuttings — scions, they are called — that are grafted to small trees in company nurseries. The scions are sections of top limbs shot down with a .22-caliber rifle. The grafts eventually yield seeds that carry the characteristics of the parent tree. In this way, the science of forestry is producing new strains of commercial trees, notably pines, to meet the growing needs of the nation and the world.

The Big Thicket area contains thousands of acres of commercial forests. These tree farms, or pine plantations, as they are known, can be seen alongside most highways in east Texas. Slash pines and loblolly pines, spaced six feet apart, grow in neat ranks and rows. When the spaces between the rows begin to fill up with brush or with other unwanted species of trees, called weed trees, a controlled burn will be scheduled to eliminate the undesirable undergrowth.

Experts make certain that the fire ignited in this potentially dangerous operation stays under control. Wet, cool days are chosen for the burn. Fire-extinguishing equipment is kept at hand. Trenches are dug around the area to be burned; they will deter flames from spreading to adjacent properties. Crews stand by to assure the containment of the fire. Thick-barked loblolly pines are relatively fire-resistant, and moist locations also help protect the loblollies and slash pines from damage. A successful burn imitates primitive nature, as when lightning set fires in the savannahs, thus eliminating invading species of plants while indigenous plants and trees survived. Nowadays the operation requires technical specialists and complex equipment to be successful. The result is a neat stand of more profitable trees, which no longer have to compete with brush for the soil's nutrients.

Many modern lumbermen realize the importance of conserving land and water resources. Wasteful practices in which bark, twigs, and other leavings of the milled lumber are trashed, belong to the past. Today's forest industry makes use of the entire tree. Even small chips from the sawed logs are processed into building materials.

The most encouraging development in decades is the increasing understanding being shown by leaders of industry toward conservation practices championed by environmentalists. The ranks of today's executives in industry include many dedicated and knowledgeable naturalists — plus managers who appreciate the national priorities placed on unique environments such as the Big Thicket. Enlightened men and women are seeking a balance between the valid desires of the environmentalists and those of commercial interests, whether forest products or oil or other industries. The past is past, and perception grows on both sides of this historic conflict.

Lumber has been the major industry of east Texas for a century, providing thousands of jobs and generating millions of dollars in profits for the companies, their investors, and for the tax coffers of the cities and towns of the area. The commercial forest, with its highly managed and renewable crops of fast-growing pines, remains inextricably linked to the economy of the Big Thicket.

The wilderness forest is a third story, actually another world. Jack Gore Baygall, largest baygall in the entire Big Thicket, provides a rugged example.

CHAPTER 13

𝄃

The Wild Forest

THE JACK GORE BAYGALL is about three miles wide and four miles long, a jungle like region where sunlight filters through one hundred-foot-tall tupelos and cypresses to reach the thick undergrowth in eerie green shafts. By night the sounds of animals moving, calling, warning others of their kind, fill the recesses of the baygall. It is the home of alligators, otters, beavers, hawks, owls, roadrunners, snakes, fox squirrels, and whitetail deer. It once reverberated with the roars of bears and howls of panthers. Oaks growing out of the muck to heights of one hundred thirty-five feet sprouted from acorns in the days when America was only a British colony. The Jack Gore Baygall is a wild piece of the Big Thicket National Preserve.

Wilderness is not an easy word to define. *Webster's New International Dictionary of the English Language* (second edition), says it is "a tract of land or a region . . . uncultivated and uninhabited by human beings." *The American Heritage Dictionary of the English Language* (New College Edition, 1981) specifies: "Any unsettled, uncultivated region left in its natural condition." Also: "A large wild tract of land covered with dense vegetation or forests." And further: "A piece of land set aside to grow wild." The United States Congress issued its own definition in the Wilderness Act: "An area where the earth and its community of life are untrammeled by man, where man himself is a visitor who does not remain." Other qualities include "outstanding opportunities for solitude or a primitive and unconfined type of recreation," and "may also contain ecological, geological, or other features of scientific, educational, scenic, or historical value."

The Jack Gore Baygall qualifies as wilderness by most of these definitions. It is not, however, untrammeled by man.

The place first became known from a native of North Carolina who came to the Big Thicket to escape possible imprisonment for injuries he inflicted on a man in a fight in Alabama. According to family accounts, "Grandpa" Gore was a well-known contestant in the footraces and fights that served as backwoods entertainment in the South before the Civil War. On one occasion, he won a race from a man known to be ill-tempered and mean. A fistfight between the two erupted. Kicking and gouging were allowed under the rustic rules, but a fighter could be taken to court and jailed if he disfigured his opponent's eyes, ears, or face. Gore was attacked viciously by his opponent and he responded in kind, almost ripping the man's eyes from their sockets. A deputy sheriff watching the fight told Gore that if he left the area he would not be punished, because nobody liked the other man and many people were glad to see him get whipped. Gore left, drifting westward. He settled on the edge of a vast baygall in the Big Thicket several years before the Civil War.

Jack Gore was the fighter's son. He was a hunter and farmer, and once owned several hundred head of cattle. (At the turn of the century, old-timers say, thousands of cattle ran loose in the area. Not until the 1950s did the Texas legislature pass laws against open-range practices. After that, cattle had to be penned up.) Descendants of Grandpa Gore and his brother, who followed the fighter to the Big Thicket, live in the area today. Numerous mailboxes on the nearby roads are marked by the name Gore.

No one lives in the baygall itself. "It's so thick that nothing don't travel in it much," Stanley Gore, Jack's son, told an interviewer. "It's just solid water in places. You would bog down in mud and water. It's a terrible place."

The baygall evolved from an ancient channel of the Neches River. Ever since the prehistoric path of the river changed course,

72

the depression has been filling up with organic matter. It drains slowly. Water oaks (*Quercus nigra*), wide-buttressed tupelos (*Nyssa aquatica*), bald cypresses (*Taxodium distichum*) compete for light in the murky depths. When a tree grows too tall for the wet soil to support, it topples. Where it stood, sunlight enters and encourages quick-growing brush, such as sweetbay magnolia (*Magnolia virginiana*) and gallberry holly (*Ilex coriacea*). Those two flourishing species gave the popular name, *baygall,* to this ecological system.

Other species massed on the edges or in the forest include yaupon (*Ilex vomitoria*), red mulberry (*Morus rubra*), water or winged elm (*Ulmus alata*), and swamp privet (*Forestiera acuminata*). They often grow in grotesque shapes, twisted from seeking the elusive slants of sunlight. Tangles of a dozen or more species of vines — rattan (*Berchemia scandens*), muscadine (*Vitis rotundifolia*), Virginia creeper (*Parthenocissus quinquefolia*), cross-vine (*Bignonia capreolata*), and others — twine the trees and underbrush together.

People who wish to explore the Jack Gore Baygall will find it on the map about twenty miles downriver from the Martin Dies, Jr., State Park. Entry to the baygall must be made by driving to the community of either Fred or Silsbee, then proceeding according to a map that may be obtained from the National Park Service in Beaumont or Woodville.

Depending on preference, one can wander for hours or days in the baygall and adjacent wilds, examining features of plant and animal life in an environment that often appears sinister. Without a compass, it is not difficult to get disoriented in these dark, swampy woods. The twilight quiet in the baygall is profound.

Hiking east toward the Neches River, one may search out key points on a topographic map: Bear Man's Bluff, Potato Patch Lake, Cocklebur Bend, Inside Prong Lake, Old Stove Bend, Gator Hole Slough, Possum Lake, Maple Slough, and Gourd Nine Eddy. The visitor will traverse elevated bluffs and hummocks, floodplain hardwood forests, lakes formed by abandoned channels of the river, and sloughs fingering inland from the broad Neches itself, in addition to the moody Jack Gore Baygall.

Man's imprint is found in parts of the 13,000 acres of the Neches Bottom and Jack Gore Baygall Unit of the Big Thicket National Preserve. Timber interests in the early years of this century felled many, if not all, of the virgin stands of magnificent hardwoods. Oil and gas wells have been drilled in some of the clearings. Yet once a visitor walks past the evidence of man's aggression, back into the forest, nature reigns. A sense of vast wilderness prevails.

"Approximately 11,000 acres of the Neches Bottom and Jack Gore Baygall Unit are designated as a wilderness objective area," states the wilderness study prepared by the National Park Service. That means that when no further oil and gas operations are possible, the existing wild places can be officially defined as wilderness: "an area . . . where man himself is a visitor who does not remain."

Any visitor who plans to stay overnight or for several days in this unit, or any other unit of the Big Thicket National Preserve, is asked to inform the National Park Service in Beaumont of his plans. If he does not return according to his itinerary, the Park Rangers may presume him lost.

CHAPTER 14

⚡

The Green Future

EMERGING from the brush bordering the western edge of the Jack Gore Baygall, a group made up of two families and their Big Thicket guide walked toward their van, then paused for a look back at the darkening trees. They had traveled over a hundred miles for a field trip in the Thicket and had spent the afternoon in the baygall, wading its sunken places and crossing its root-bound hummocks.

"I'm glad to be out of that place and back in the open space," confessed one member of the party, peeling a large silver-backed chestnut oak leaf from his sweat-damp shirt.

"Surprised to hear you say that," commented another. "That's one of the most peaceful and fascinating places I've ever been. I'm ready to come back tomorrow!"

Their guide nodded. Reactions to the wild places in the Thicket are often mixed. Many people who visit the Thicket feel comfortable in spots where humans control nature, such as the recreational and commercial forests, but uncomfortable where nature is left unimpeded. And vice versa.

The future of the Big Thicket in the units of the national preserve favors those who are willing to let nature have its own way. The rest of the region will be developed.

Not much of the original wilderness was saved, less than 3 percent of the primitive 3.5 million acres. And that barely in time. Yet 84,550 acres were saved. Every other acre in east Texas may eventually give way to development and "progress," but the Big Thicket National Preserve will evolve on nature's own timetable, according to its patterns and peculiarities, with minimal interference from humans. That special condition was never granted by the U.S. government before.

Exploration for minerals is permitted, but only in consonance with extremely rigid regulations set by the National Park Service and monitored by highly trained Rangers.

As the custodian of the twelve units of this sanctuary, the National Park Service is dedicated to the meaning of *preserve*. Even when the Rangers set out a trail in one of the units, it is little more than a path about three feet wide, melding into leaf-littered woods. When they build a bridge over a creek or a walkway over an extremely sensitive plant community, such as an orchid-strewn seep in a wetlands savannah, the structure is natural and simple.

In addition to having the preserve accessible at all seasons of the year, visitors participate in Park Service activities that cover virtually every facet of Big Thicket nature. Every weekend, naturalists offer programs suited to the season — from canoeing, birding, foraging for wild foods, and discovering the night life of the forest (a woods walk with flashlight to discover the habits of nocturnal creatures), to daylong interpretive hikes along Turkey Creek and learning to explore wild places with only a compass. Special activities for children, such as utilizing the patterns of nature for homemade Christmas cards, are offered in holiday seasons.

Preserve, Observe, Enjoy — these might be the watchwords of the future in the National Preserve, a far cry from the waste and destruction that marked much of the past.

Meanwhile, day by day, the woods and meadows in the twelve protected units of the preserve return to the freedom of primeval epochs. The original Big Thicket will never be duplicated, of course. Nor would nature care to repeat itself. At any given moment and place wilderness is changing, proliferating, creating, and re-creating. That process is the unending promise of a green future in the preserve. The crucial difference today is that man is now the guest of nature here, no longer its tyrant. Instead of interfering, he observes, absorbs, learns.

Much of the Big Thicket's pristine grandeur will return, perhaps even more intense and elaborate than its present richness. Nature fairly leaps at the chance to recover, reseed, and renew itself. Even today in some sunny recess, another Witness Tree magnolia grows toward its thousandth year of life, and beyond.

Acknowledgments

In one way or in many ways, the following persons made distinguished or delightful contributions to this telling of the story of the Big Thicket: Kenneth R. Bryan, James and Connie Clark, Nina Cullinan, former U.S. Representative Bob Eckhardt, Wood Fain, John and Doretta Gilchrist, Frank Lively, Miron and Marjorie Love, Downs Matthews, Harold Nicholas, Ed Poulsen, Emmit and Mae Tuggle, former U.S. Senator Ralph W. Yarborough. I am particularly indebted to Howard N. Martin for his scholarly counsel and criticism on portions of the story dealing with the Alabama and Coushatta Indians.

For aid, support, and encouragement in the research and writing of the story, I am further indebted to: Ab Abernethy, Frank Abraham, Gerrie Andrews, Saul Aranow, A.R.E. group 16, Phebe and Dan Armstrong, Laura Assunto, W. V. "Smoke" Ballew, Preston Barnes, Bleu Bethard, Buddy Beck, Pat and Eleanor Blair, Maurice Blonstein, Bob Boykin, Bill Brett, Virginia Bullock, Gayle Burton, the late Hugh Lynn Cayce, the loan committee of the Citizens State Bank, Rodney Cook, Teresa Cook, Martha Corson, Kelly Craine, Bill and Alicia Cromie, Don and Nancy Joy Dedera, Charlie Dillingham, Pep and Nancy Fertitta, Archer Fullingim, John and the late Jan Gagliano, Gus and Beth Galiano, Nick and Cora Gerren, Dee Gibson, Leon Hale, Martin Houston, Ruth Houston, Janeece Hudson, Edward and Beechie Hutcheson, Bob Jirsa, Shirley Jones, Bruce Kleinman, Lorraine Leavell, the library staff

79

in Woodville, Texas, Joan Loiodice, Mike and Virginia Lloyd, B. J. Lowe, Tom Lubbert, William H. Matthews III, Sally Matuskey, Maury and Julia Maverick, Jerry and Kaffy Mize, George Anne Monger, Bob Mosbacher, John and Doris Neibel, James Nelson (PhotoGraphics), the Nichols Clinic, Nadya Olyanova, Rick Ostler, Jimmie and Corita Owen, Joe and Asako Peacock, W. W. "Bill" Phillips, Jr., Dayton and Jean Pickett, Tommie Pinkard, Ashley Poindexter, the postal workers of Woodville, Ralph and Laine Potter, Eugenia Rayzor, Steve Richard, Ann Roberts, Carter and Eloise Rochelle, Eduard Muegge "Buck" Schiwetz, Helen Schmalz, the late Jack Shofner, Mary Jean Shofner, Joe Siblo, Jill Spurlock, Otis Thomas, Merritt Thomas, Johnny and Esther Walker, Katy White, and Jack Zilker.

I cast a kiss on the east breeze to my unseen editors, Karen Klockner and Jean Crockett, for unfailing cheerfulness and help-fulness, and for unflinching insistence on high literary standards.

I am warmly grateful to all.

Howard Peacock

Bibliography and Further Reading

Abernethy, Francis Edward. *Tales From The Big Thicket.* Austin: University of Texas Press, 1966.

Ajilvsgi, Geyata. *Wild Flowers of the Big Thicket, East Texas, and Western Louisiana.* College Station, Texas: Texas A&M University Press, 1979.

American Heritage, Eds. *Natural Wonders.* (Alvin M. Josephy, Jr., editor in charge). American Heritage, 1963.

Aronow, Saul. *Notes on the Geologic Units.* Beaumont, Texas: Department of Geology, Lamar University, 1981.

The Original Water-Color Paintings by John James Audubon for the Birds of America (original paintings in the collection of the New York Historical Society), American Heritage, 1966. Introduction by Marshall B. Davidson.

Bernard, H. A., and R. J. LeBlanc. "Résumé of the Quaternary Geology of the Northwestern Gulf of Mexico Province," in *The Quaternary of the United States.* Princeton, New Jersey: Princeton University Press, 1965.

Big Thicket Bulletin (Saratoga, Texas): No. 41 (Sept. 1977), articles by Dr. William A. Owens, John Watson, Elizabeth Woods, Jim Clark, Judy Allen, Bill Brett; No. 47 (March 1978), article by Howard Peacock; No. 50 (June 1978), article by Bill Hollomon and Maxine Johnston.

Brown, Clair A. *Wildflowers of Louisiana and Adjoining States*. Baton Rouge: Louisiana State University Press, 1972.

Correll, Donovan S., and Helen B. Correll. *Aquatic and Wetland Plants of the Southwestern United States*. Washington, D.C.: Environmental Protection Agency, 1972.

Cozine, James. "Assault on a Wilderness." Ph.D. dissertation (1976).

Davis, William B. *The Mammals of Texas*. Austin, Texas: Texas Parks and Wildlife Department, 1966.

Dobie, J. Frank. *The Ben Lilly Legend*. Boston: Little, Brown, 1950.

Douglas, William O. *Farewell to Texas: A Vanishing Wilderness*. New York: McGraw-Hill, 1967.

Eckholm, Erik P. *Disappearing Species: the Social Challenge*. Washington: Worldwatch Institute, 1978.

France, Ghillean T. and Thomas S. Elias, eds., *Extinction is Forever: Proceedings of a Symposium*. Bronx, New York: New York Botanical Garden, 1977.

Gunter, Pete. *The Big Thicket*. Austin and New York: Jenkins, 1971.

Hofferbert, Louis. *Unlikely Critters of the Big Thicket*. Museum Publication Series, No. 4. Saratoga, Texas: Big Thicket Museum, 1973.

Johnston, Maxine, ed. *Thicket Explorer*, Museum Publication Series, No. 3. Saratoga, Texas: Big Thicket Museum, 1972.

Lasswell, Mary. *I'll Take Texas*. Boston: Houghton Mifflin, 1958.

Matthews, William H., III. *Texas Fossils*. Austin: Bureau of Economic Geology, University of Texas, 1960.

McLeod, Claude A. *The Big Thicket of East Texas*. Huntsville, Texas: Sam Houston Press, 1967.

National Park Service. *Visitor Use/General Development, Big Thicket National Preserve*. Beaumont, Texas: 1977.

Newcomb, W. W., Jr. *The Indians of Texas from Prehistoric to Modern Times*. Austin: University of Texas Press, 1961.

Peacock, Howard, ed. *The Big Thicket — Participants Handbook for The Contemporary Science Seminar, Spring 1974.* Houston, Texas: Houston Museum of Natural Science and University of Houston, 1974.

Peacock, Howard, ed. *The Big Thicket — Participants Handbook for the Contemporary Science Seminar, Fall 1975.* Houston, Texas: Houston Museum of Natural Science and University of Houston, 1975.

Peterson, Roger Tory, and the editors of Time-Life Books. *The Birds.* New York: Time-Life Books, 1963.

Sargent, Charles Sprague. *Manual of the Trees of North America.* 2 vols., New York: Dover Publications, Inc., 1961 (Republication of 1922 original edition.)

Vines, Robert A. *Trees, Shrubs and Woody Vines of the Southwest.* Austin: University of Texas Press, 1960.

Watson, Geraldine. *Big Thicket Plant Ecology, An Introduction.* Museum Publication Series, No. 5. Saratoga, Texas: Big Thicket Museum, 1975.

Index

scions, 68
seeps, 6
Silsbee, Texas, 73
Six Shooter Kate, 47
snakes, vii, xiii, 11
sore eyes, 40–41
Sour Lake boom, 42
Sour Lake, Texas, 46, 48
Southern Pacific Railroad, 32
Spain / Spanish, 21, 22–23:
  -French war, 18, 21–22
  war with Texas, 23
spinal meningitis, 41
Spindletop oil well / field, 42–46
staggerbush, 12
strawberry bush, 5
stream floodplain ecosystem, 11
stretchberry, 35
sumac, flame-leaf, 36
sundew (*Drosera*), 3, 6, 12
swamps, vii, xiii, 11. *See also* baygalls
swamp privet (*Forestiera acuminata*), 73
sweetbriar, 14

tapir, 15
Tennessee, 26
Texas, 17, 22, 26:
  bear territory of, 53
  French-Spanish war over, 21–22
  lumber industry in, 69–70
  purchase of Big Thicket by, 24
  support of Confederacy, 31
  war of independence from Mexico, 23–24
  war with Spain, 23
Texas and New Orleans Railroad, 32
Texas Rangers, 47
Thoreau, Henry David, 5–6
titi thickets, 11

Tonkawa Indians, 17
Topeka State Journal, 49
Trinity River, 16, 23
Trinity and Sabine Railroad, 32
tupelo:
  water, 11
  wide-buttressed (*Nyssa aquatica*), 73
turkey, wild, 19, 27
Turkey Creek, 76

Union Wells Creek, viii
U.S. Biological Survey, 50

Venus's-flytrap, 3
Village Creek, viii, ix, xiii, xv
Virginia creeper (*Parthenocissus quinquefolia*), 73

wahoo bush (*Euonymous americanus*), 5
Watson, Geraldine, 12–13, 65
weed trees, 68
whooping crane, 57
Wichita Indians, 17
Willis Formation, 16
Wilson, Alexander, 55
Wilson, Charles, 65
Witness Tree, 63–64, 77
Wolf Gully, viii
woodpecker:
  ivory-billed, 10–11, 57–58
  king, 58
  red-cockaded, 10
Woodville, Texas, 66, 73
Woodwell, George M., 58

Yarborough, Ralph W., 64
yaupon (*Ilex vomitoria*), 73
Yearling Tick Branch, viii
yucca, Spanish bayonet, xiii, xiv